MORGAN PHILLIPS
Labour Party Secretary

MORGAN PHILLIPS

Labour Party Secretary

By Morgan Phillips

Edited by Morgan D Phillips

Cover designed by Catherine Phillips

SPOKESMAN
Nottingham

First published in 2017 by
Spokesman for Labour Heritage
Russell House
Bulwell lane
Nottingham NG6 0BT
England

Phone 0115 9708318
Fax 0115 9420433
www.spokesmanbooks.com

A catalogue record is available from the British Library.

ISBN 978 0 85124 867 7

Printed in Nottingham by Russell Press (www.russellpress.com)

CONTENTS

Appendix

FOREWORD
Stan Newens

The Labour Party was founded as the Labour Representation Committee at a conference called by the Trade Union Congress in February 1900 at the Memorial Hall in London

It first contested a General Election in 1902, but won only two seats in Parliament. In the General Election of 1906, it was better organised and, by means of an agreement with the Liberal Party, returned 29 Members of Parliament. It grew gradually in the following years and, in the decade which followed the 1ˢᵗ World War, it was able, with Liberal Party support, to form minority governments in 1923 and again in 1929 – both led by Ramsay MacDonald.

However, in 1931, following the economic crisis which began in 1929, Ramsay MacDonald dismissed his Cabinet when it refused to support drastic cuts in public expenditure, and formed a coalition with Liberals and Conservatives. In the General Election which followed in 1931, Labour suffered a catastrophic defeat, losing 140 seats. Reduced to 49 MPs, it appeared to be on the way to oblivion and of no lasting significance.

Despite this, however, the party made a modest recovery in the 1935 General Election. As no more General Elections were held for 10 years, owing to the outbreak of the Second World War, there was no opportunity before 1945 to recover lost ground. In 1945, following the final defeat of Nazi Germany, a General Election was called and all the main political parties girded themselves for the fray.

In 1944, Jim Middleton, who had served for 41 years as Assistant Secretary and then Secretary of the Labour Party, retired and the National Executive Committee (NEC) chose as his successor Morgan Phillips, a former Welsh miner, who had won a scholarship to follow a two year course at the Labour College in Earls Court. Phillips had worked as a Labour Party Organiser and had served as Secretary of the Party's Research Department at Transport House since 1941. Once his appointment had been confirmed by the Party's annual conference, on 12 December 1944, he took overall control of what turned out to be a momentous and historic campaign. Less than a year later, on 5 July 1945, the British electorate returned Labour to power with a majority of 180 over the Conservatives and 146 over all other parties.

Morgan Phillips' success, which was due primarily to taking over at a key moment, placed him in a powerful position, not only over the Labour Party's organisation, but one from which he could influence important political decisions. His autobiography gives his account of how he saw the situation developing and reflects his wish to carry out faithfully what the Party decided democratically. His comments on Clement Attlee, Ernest Bevin, Harold Laski and the far-reaching, radical changes achieved by the Labour Government are of interest to all historians.

After the Government's majority was drastically cut back to six by the 1950 General Election, Morgan Phillips, along with Herbert Morrison, tried to persuade Clement Attlee to delay the following General Election until Labour's standing with the electorate improved. Their advice was ignored with the result that, despite achieving most votes, Labour lost the 1951 General Election and the Conservatives were returned with a majority of 17.

Labour's electoral prospects were undoubtedly damaged by Aneurin Bevan's refusal to accept certain changes imposed on the National Health Service by the Chancellor of the Exchequer, Hugh Gaitskell, to pay for an increase in the expenditure on arms. The split in the Government was escalated by the resignation of Harold Wilson and John Freeman along with Bevan.

Morgan Phillips gives his inside account of the dispute which became a major feature of Labour politics in the 1950s. Although he was regarded by most rank and file left-wingers at the time as a committed right-winger, for carrying out decisions of the right-wing majority on NEC, he reveals, not only that he kept in touch with Aneurin Bevan as a friend, but also that he held him in high esteem.

When Bevan opposed Hugh Gaitskell's idea of dropping Clause IV of the Constitution at the 1959 Labour Party Conference, in Morgan Phillips' view, 'this truly great man' made 'the finest and most important speech of his career'.

Morgan Philips suffered a stroke in 1961 which forced him to resign as General Secretary in 1962. Over the period in which he held this position (1944 – 1962) he not only oversaw the Party's domestic organisation, but took a close interest in international affairs and the reconstitution of the Socialist International after the Second World War. This is the subject of a separate section of his autobiography.

Philips began meeting socialists from other countries from October 1944, when he went to Paris to attend a Congress of the French Socialist Party. Subsequently, he met representatives from numerous countries.

However, any hope of having a single international organisation to include Communist representatives from Eastern Europe soon fell apart.

Subsequently, the persecution of socialists in East European countries under Communist control was a continuing problem, and the Labour Party banned all links with the Communist Parties in Britain and in Europe. Morgan Phillips was a hardliner on this issue, although this did not prevent him from enjoying good relations with President Tito of Yugoslavia, after he broke with the Soviet Union. However, this did not survive when the regime put on trial prominent Communists such as Milovan Djilas.

In the post-war world, the clash with Communism led Morgan Phillips to support the alliance of Western nations against the Soviets. He argued that British socialism owed more to religious organisations like Methodism than to Marxism.

Although his views would not be shared by many Labour Party activists and thinkers, his contribution to the movement was considerable and should not be underestimated. As he relates in this autobiography, he originated from a mining working class community and having experienced unemployment and poverty, dedicated his life to the task of improving conditions for all through the Labour Party. The story of his life is a significant contribution to the history of our movement in the 20th Century and, as such, Labour Heritage is proud to publish it.

Part 1

Labour Party Secretary
by
Morgan Phillips

A visit to Winston Churchill

On Wednesday the 22nd March 1944 the National Executive Committee of the Labour Party held interviews for the senior post of General Secretary. The six short-listed candidates each made a brief statement and then answered questions. After two ballots only the newspaperman Maurice Webb and I, Morgan Phillips, the Party's Research Secretary, were left in contention.

Maurice was deservedly popular with his fellow journalists, who were very surprised and in many ways disappointed when I emerged successful from the third ballot. As AJ Cummings put it in the News Chronicle:

'In appointing one of its departmental officials to the important office of Secretary, the Labour Party seems to have decided deliberately against the choice of a political personality.... Time will show if there is any wisdom in this or whether it is just another sign that Labour has got into an interminable rut.'

The Constitution laid down that I could not take up my duties until the Party's Annual Conference approved my appointment. This was planned for May in the Central Hall, Westminster, but it was postponed, ostensibly because London was being subjected to heavy doodlebug raids. The unstated reason for the postponement was the Government's wish to curtail civilian travel during the build-up to the D-Day invasion of early June.

The War was rapidly moving towards its conclusion, and the unity of the United Kingdom's Coalition Government was subject to many strains. Every year the Government had to have a Prolongation of Parliament Bill. It was the job of the Minister of Home Security (Herbert Morrison) to introduce this. By October 1944 because of the encouraging progress in the War there was a great deal of Conservative resistance to prolonging the coalition and indeed the Parliament. Herbert Morrison too was raring to get back to party politics. The Labour Movement as a whole felt that the Coalition was lagging behind in its plans for post-war reconstruction.

Labour's Annual Conference eventually took place in the week beginning 11th December 1944. My appointment was confirmed on the second day and I started my duties immediately. The proceedings ran from 9.30 am to 6 pm and when they finished many of us adjourned to the St Ermin's Hotel, where we were running a conference each evening for socialists from the liberated countries of Europe. It was a very heavy week.

Delegates to the Labour Conference felt particularly uneasy about the situation in Greece, where British troops might be used to restore the monarchy and to support the centrist General Plastiras against EAM/ELAS, who had played such a magnificent part in resisting the Nazis. Aware of the delegates' disaffection the National Executive tabled a resolution urging the Coalition Government to do everything possible to secure an armistice and to establish talks leading to a provisional Greek government and a free general election. Arthur Greenwood moved this resolution, but Ernest Bevin, the Coalition's Minister of Labour, defended the Government's policy:

> 'These steps which have been taken in Greece are not the decision of Winston Churchill, they are the decisions of the cabinet.'

He reminded Conference that Britain had demanded a provisional Greek government involving the six main parties including ELAS, and had offered to provide food and security if all those participating in the new government gave their agreement.

> 'Every party signed, and it was on that agreement and that signature that we went into Greece … We never expected ELAS or any other of the armed bands to go back on this agreement.'

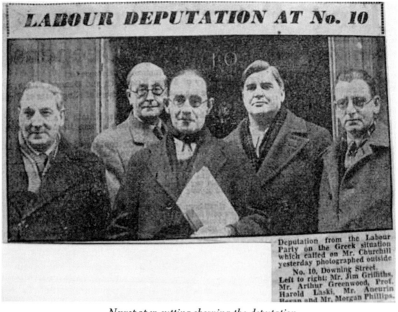

Newspaper cutting showing the deputation

Fierce opposition came from Nye Bevan. He asked the Conference to condemn the Government's action, and to insist that Labour ministers either exercise a more decisive socialist influence or else leave the Tories to do their own dirty work.

After the Conference had approved the Executive's resolution, we had to decide how to bring its contents to the notice of the Prime Minister. Mr Churchill agreed to meet a delegation on the 15th January 1945, so Harold Laski, Jim Griffiths, Arthur Greenwood, Nye Bevan and I gathered at 10 Downing Street and were immediately ushered into the Cabinet Room. The Prime Minister soon joined us, took one look at Nye Bevan and clearly showed that he was not pleased to see any of us, least of all Nye. Churchill offered nothing in the way of preliminaries and sat there mute, listening to our representations.

Eventually Arthur Greenwood provoked him into breaking his silence, and Churchill at great length outlined opinions which were largely the same as those expressed at the Conference by Ernest Bevin. The atmosphere relaxed enormously. Though we did not share his desire for the restoration of the Greek monarchy, there was general consent on the need for free and fair elections. To make this possible the Labour Party released Dick Windle, the Party's Assistant National Agent, to lead a team of experienced Labour, Conservative and Liberal agents, who would compile a register in Greece to facilitate a referendum and elections.

* * *

The Harold Laski affair

Once Winston Churchill had promised not to seek a further prolongation of Parliament beyond 1944, a General Election before October 1945 became inevitable. At my first meeting of Labour's National Executive I proposed a campaign committee made up of some of the chairmen from the Party's 27 sub-committees. It would need the authority to make decisions and to take emergency action if necessary. My proposal was accepted and a committee formed of Hugh Dalton, Arthur Greenwood, Harold Laski, Herbert Morrison, George Shepherd, Ellen Wilkinson, Tom Williamson, Barbara Gould and myself.

We had to decide on the number of leaflets, posters and pamphlets that we intended to publish so that we could negotiate with the Board of Trade for the necessary amount of paper, which was then severely rationed. Our main task was to prepare a short policy statement that would form the basis of an election manifesto to be discussed at the forthcoming Party Conference (Whitsun 1945 in Blackpool). From the 27 sub-committee reports we tried to establish priorities and to compile a cohesive and comprehensive programme capable of fulfilment within one Parliament.

Discussions went fairly smoothly. The main controversy was over the nationalisation of the steel industry. Herbert Morrison was reluctant, Hugh Dalton enthusiastic. The battle waged backwards and forwards but in the end Dalton persuaded the majority of his colleagues, despite Morrison's long and spirited rear-guard action. The policy statement was published as a pamphlet 'Let Us Face the Future'. It was very well received, and it sold more than 1,750,000 copies.

On the 7th May 1945, two days after the German surrender, the Party's National Executive called a special meeting to discuss whether Labour should continue participating in the Coalition Government until the defeat of Japan or should press for an autumn general election. Bevin agreed with Churchill but did not press his opinions. Hardly anyone believed that the ten year old Parliament could extend its life now that the War in Europe had ended. We wanted a general election.

Eleven days after the Executive meeting, when we were in Blackpool preparing for the Annual Conference, I received a phone message. The Party Leader Clem Attlee was on his way with a letter from the Prime Minister, which need to be discussed with the Labour members of the Coalition (Bevin, Morrison, Dalton, Ellen Wilkinson and Philip Noel Baker). Attlee wanted me to attend also. The meeting took place around 10 pm. It transpired that Churchill had rejected the idea of an autumn election. He wanted Parliament prolonged until after a decisive victory over Japan and he even suggested a national referendum on prolongation.

After a two hour meeting Attlee formulated his reply, which he intended to send subject to the approval of the National Executive and of Conference. It was strongly worded:

> 'I do not think it would be either right or possible to obtain from Parliament another prolongation of its life. I could not consent to the introduction into our national life of a device so alien to all our traditions as the referendum, which has only too often been the instrument of Nazism and Fascism.'

Two days later Churchill visited King George VI to tender his Government's resignation. Polling day was fixed for the 5th July. In the meantime the Conservatives acted as a caretaker government.

The Labour Party Conference had already heard speeches from the platform that were as confident as they were constructive. Ellen Wilkinson (the retiring Chairman of the National Executive), Herbert Morrison and Hugh Dalton all excelled themselves. Then, on the day that Churchill announced the end of the Coalition, Ernest Bevin made an unforgettable speech on foreign affairs, an address which was to have far-reaching consequences for him. He exuded confidence of a big Labour victory. Indeed when the Conference ended everyone departed in high spirits. In my whole career I have never seen such optimism. It was a pleasure to visit Labour committee rooms in every part of the country. The public was behind us, meetings were well attended and the campaign seemed to be going our way. Then came the Laski affair.

Churchill, the caretaker Prime Minister, was due to meet Stalin and the American President Harry Truman in Berlin, and he invited Clem Attlee, the Labour leader, to accompany him. Harold Laski told a *Daily Herald* reporter that Attlee should attend as an observer only, and not participate in the discussions. This intervention was particularly embarrassing as Laski now held the Chairmanship of Labour's National Executive, and he could be regarded as speaking for the Labour Party. I contacted him at once to see if he had been misreported. In reply he sent me a three page hand-written document which he hoped to present to the National Executive. (Part of it is reprinted in an appendix to this book.) Basically, he did not want the Labour Party to be bound by decisions made in secret discussions involving Winston Churchill.

I managed to dissuade him from showing his letter to the Executive and I hoped the matter would blow over. Unfortunately, Churchill sought to interpret Laski's reported remarks as an attempt by the Labour Party to dictate to a future Prime Minister, an interpretation to which Clem Attlee took great exception. He pointed out:

> 'The Chairman has not the power to give me instructions nor do his remarks to a Press correspondent constitute the official authoritative and reiterated instructions of the Executive Committee of the Labour Party.'

When Churchill persisted, Attlee delivered a telling rebuke:

> 'I think that you underestimate the intelligence of the public.'

The Tory press did their utmost to exploit the situation. Headlines conveyed that Attlee, if elected, would be a mere puppet dancing to Laski's tune. Naturally Attlee was annoyed because Laski's indiscretion was playing into the Tories' hands. This created a problem for me, as the

Party Constitution required the election manifesto to be signed by the Chairman of the National Executive (i.e. Harold Laski). In my view, Laski's signature would add fuel to the fire already started by the Tory press. It would be prudent to ignore the Party constitution and have Clem Attlee's signature alone.

Attlee and Laski both agreed with me, though Herbert Morrison dissented. When I called a meeting in my office to finalise the manifesto, Morrison and (at my suggestion) Laski stayed away. Harold was the most helpful and co-operative person that I have ever worked with. The manifesto was then issued with Attlee's signature alone.

In a radio broadcast Churchill started throwing out accusations of a Labour Gestapo. It engendered much resentment because it was so untrue. Churchill had that combative instinct, which made him such a great leader in wartime. When he was in a fight his language got increasingly colourful. The whole anti-Laski campaign made little impact on the voters. Attlee was right; the Conservatives had underestimated people's intelligence. The Party Conference may lay down the general lines of policy but it cannot dictate to a Labour Government. Still less can the Chairman of the National Executive.

* * *

General Election 1945

Rather than early July, I would have preferred the General Election to be held in October 1945. By that time a large number of troops would be back in Britain and an effective Electoral Register could be compiled. We would have been able to hold a Whitsun Conference to discuss our policy document 'Let Us Face the Future'. However, Churchill opted for July. As far as we were concerned the fight was on, and the best thing to do was to get on with it. For example, we had a large number of candidates to find in a hurry. We had to bring some back from the forces overseas. They could wear civilian clothes for the campaign. We had to ensure that every constituency had a candidate. Then we arranged our ability to respond to requests for information, coming from candidates, voters and the press. In the 1945 election there were pressure groups on issues like friendly societies, social insurance, war pensions, anti-vivisection. We planned tours for leading members covering as much of the country as possible and making authoritative statements.

My office also had to negotiate our allocation of paper and petrol for the campaign. In the political broadcasts on BBC radio we helped speakers with information and background material, and made sure that the talks were complementary and not duplicating each other. Ernest Bevin had an office in Transport House on the floor above mine, and I clearly remember him working on a speech to be broadcast during the campaign. He showed me a copy and I told him it was too long for the time allowed. We agreed on areas where cuts could be made but often there was a snag. He would say, 'I like that little bit. If I go a bit quicker I can keep it in, can't I?' The speech was still too long but it came over very well.

Clement Attlee liked to sit at his typewriter and type his own speeches, using just one or two fingers. Seeing how busy he was in the campaign, I composed a script that might be helpful. When I took it to him at the Midland Hotel Manchester his wife read it and said, 'But that's not Clem.' He promptly sat down and typed his own.

Only those who were present in Britain during 1945 can appreciate the tremendous effort made by the Conservative Party and its allies to present the election as an occasion for expressing gratitude to Winston Churchill for his war leadership. This line was pursued by the Conservatives at the expense of a full exposition of their policy. There were also prodigious newspaper and radio efforts to discredit the leadership of the Labour Party. With ample funds and the greater part of the national press behind it, the Conservative Party covered the nation day after day with its election propaganda. However, we began to see signs that all was not well. There were stirrings among the people who, although paying their full mead of tribute to Churchill for his magnificent war efforts, were not prepared to place their future in the hands of his Party. They could not easily forget the tragedy of the inter-war years – unemployment, short time, low wages, malnutrition and the constant atmosphere of internal and international strife. During the war they had seen the state plan for its survival using bulk purchases, concentration of industry and the selection of priorities. Labour's propaganda was spelling out the need for the state to plan for the organisation of a satisfactory peace. Conservative policy was in essence a plea for a return to the anarchy, chaos and insecurity of the 1920s and 1930s.

Local Labour groups, regional organisations, headquarters staff at Transport House, together with thousands of voluntary workers, were busy fighting the election campaign with energy and enthusiasm. Volunteers addressed meetings across the country. Thousands canvassed door to door urging voters to exercise their rights of self-expression. I was working 14 or 15 hours a day, seven days a week. At weekends I did meetings in the provinces to keep in contact and find out the prevailing mood.

Polling day, the 5th July 1945, found the Party confident of victory. All our workers, even in Tory strongholds like Warwick and Leamington, believed that Labour would win.

Unfortunately, the ballot boxes were not to be opened until the 25th July to allow the votes of servicemen overseas time to reach the United Kingdom. The first of these three intervening weeks was bearable because I involved myself in the 'little election' – constituencies which had delayed voting because Election Day coincided with holidays or wakes weeks. Despite conflicting rumours and speculation I remained confident of a big Labour victory, as Bill Barclay later testified in the *Daily Express*:

> 'Mr Morgan Phillips gave me the result of the General Election in 1945 a few days before it was held. If I had accepted his figures I should have been regarded as a celebrated prophet. He was only about ten seats out. But I laughed at him then.'

Finally the 25th arrived, the ballot boxes were opened and the votes counted. We did not have to wait long. The first result showed a Labour gain in Salford South. Minutes later we heard that Harold Macmillan, the Secretary of State for Air in the caretaker government, and another leading Tory Brendan Bracken had been defeated.

The next morning, party workers and others began to gather in Transport Hall (on the ground floor of our headquarters Transport House, Westminster) for the results to be flashed onto a screen. I went for lunch at the Ivy Restaurant with Herbert Tracey, Chief Publicity Officer of the Trades Union Congress, who had helped me throughout the campaign. The proprietor gave us a private corner complete with radio so that we could hear the latest results. Needless to say this was a very pleasant lunch.

Returning to my office I found Clem Attlee there with his wife and family. There were so many people there that eventually we moved to Ernest Bevin's office. At 3.30 pm a hand-written message arrived for Attlee from Winston Churchill. Clem placed it on the table for us to read. Churchill conceded a Labour victory, offered congratulations, and announced that he was proceeding to the Palace, to tender his resignation and recommend to His Majesty that Attlee be invited to form a new government.

It was a great victory. We had 393 MPs with 11,992,292 votes. The

Conservatives had 198 MPs with 9,058,020 votes. There were 49 MPs representing other parties but our overall majority was huge. Everyone felt that this was the start of the millennium. As party workers celebrated at the Marquis of Granby opposite Transport House, there was no thought of the difficulties that would face the elected government, no realisation that ration books, restrictions and control would still be needed in the post-war world.

* * *

A Bargoed Childhood

Labour's great victory in 1945 occurred shortly after my 43rd birthday. I was born on the 18th June 1902 in the small but politically progressive mining town of Aberdare, South Wales. It was a double-member constituency and one of the MPs was James Keir Hardie, the great pioneer of the Labour Movement. My mother was a member of the Independent Labour Party and my father, who had started in the mines at the age of nine, was a militant trade unionist. Soon after I was born we moved to the newer mining town of Bargoed in the Rhymney Valley. In time, I attended the Infants and then the elementary School. I do not recall much except that I did all that was expected of me, passed my examinations and advanced to a new form each year. My clearest impression from that period is of rushing home on Coronation Day 1910, falling down and breaking a commemorative mug given by a benevolent local authority. I also remember the street football matches that always ended in a free-for-all. In the 1910 General Election I wore the colours of the Independent Labour Party candidate CB Stanton, and became embroiled in a street fight. Stanton came bottom of the poll but I won my scrap.

On Sundays my grandmother Mary Jones ensured that I attended the local Wesleyan chapel in the morning, afternoon and evening. The influence exerted on me then has not been destroyed, even though in later life I attended for two years the only full-time Marxist training institution in the United Kingdom.

In January 1915 I passed the Labour Examination, which allowed me to leave school, whereupon I became an errand boy for the Home & Colonial grocery stores. I worked twelve hours a day Monday-Wednesday, seven on Thursday (early closing), thirteen on Friday and seventeen on Saturday (parcel delivery day). Every morning I had to scrub the shop floor. All this for the princely sum of eight shillings a week.

As my fourteenth birthday approached I realised that instead of eight I could earn fifteen shillings if I entered the coalmine. This I did, despite the opposition of my parents.

My first job was to clear away a fallen roof, and I vividly remember trying to shovel between the rails and the sleepers. It was exhausting and frustrating and, but for my stubbornness, I would have gone back to my job at the grocer's. Gradually I became accustomed to the work, and when I was old enough I attended evening classes to study mining and economics. One of my tutors, Harold Watkins, an active socialist, planned debates from which I and other students benefitted greatly. Many years later in his book *Unusual Students* (Brython Press, 1947) he recalled a conference of eighty students drawn from the various centres in Glamorgan, where he was Adult Education Tutor, and generously praised my contribution:

> 'His method was to reduce the (opposing) argument to absurdity by ridicule and irony and by appeal to facts and experience. His diction was smooth, his vocabulary extraordinarily rich, his voice deep and strong, and occasionally he would coin a brilliant epigram.'

Throughout this time the mining industry was in ferment with frequent disputes between employers and men. At seventeen I joined the Independent Labour Party and became active in trade union matters. The First World War had ended, but a great deal of jingoism remained. I well remember a local election in 1920 when the Labour candidate Morgan Jones, who taught in my old school, was bitterly attacked by ex-servicemen's organisations because of his pacifist activities and propaganda during the War. Our meetings were broken up, stones were thrown and the windows of the ILP rooms shattered. Jones lost, but a year later many of the same people lustily cheered his victory in a Parliamentary by-election. He went on to be a Parliamentary under Secretary in the first Labour Government (1924).

To earn a little more money I became a part-time stagehand, operating the limelight and later the switchboard, carrying the 'props' in on Monday mornings and out again on Saturday nights. Sometimes I had the exciting experience of walking onstage with the Chinese conjuror Chung Ling Soo or the electrical wizard Dr Walford Bodie. Years later, when I mentioned this at the Annual Conference of the National Association of Theatrical and Kine Employees, they made me an honorary member of the union.

The Unemployed Association

We were working short time in the mines because of the ever-growing economic crisis. On the 12ᵗʰ March 1921 I received my first dismissal notice, together with all the men and boys in our colliery. A group of us formed a committee to set up an unemployed association. I was made secretary for the simple reason that I was the youngest member.

The committee discussed the idea of a march to the Merthyr Board of Guardians. I took this seriously and immediately wrote to the Clerk of the Guardians asking when they would be willing to receive a delegation. A few days later I was very pleased to receive a reply stating a date ten days ahead. I proudly carried this to the next committee meeting only to have my enthusiasm dashed when the others pointed out that we had not even begun to recruit members for our association. Fortunately they were men of great loyalty, imagination and courage and they started recruiting at once rather than let me down.

First they organised meetings, asking me to address the initial gathering at 10.30 the following morning. I spent the rest of that day preparing and memorising a speech which included demands for the opening of more Relief Offices, higher rates of relief, and shoes and clothing for miners' children. When the family had gone to bed I practised my speech and timed myself by the clock; it would last 25 minutes.

Next morning I arrived at the meeting place, a small recreation ground at Pontlottyn surrounded by houses. When I got up to speak I was so nervous that I could not see the audience before me. I started with 'Mr Chairman' and I could have sworn that somebody repeated my words. That sensation remained with me throughout the speech making me more and more nervous. I did not realise that the echo of my voice was being thrown back by the houses surrounding the ground.

At last the ordeal came to an end. I checked to see how long I had spoken, only to find that I had rushed through my carefully prepared 25 minute speech in eight or nine minutes. Even so, my hearers were generous in their applause. Despite my shortcomings as secretary we recruited 600 sympathisers and the demonstration took place as planned. All 600 of us marched twelve-and-a-half miles to the meeting of the Board of Guardians. When we arrived the Board offered us each a cup of water and a piece of bread and cheese.

I made one unfortunate mistake on the march. I organised a collection en route, ignorant of the fact that police permission was necessary. The day after the march the chairman and I were warned that we had broken the law. This led to a long and protracted correspondence but we escaped prosecution.

When the national lockout started, our activities merged with those of the main organisation. My colleagues and I were more fortunate than others because we received unemployment pay, but our good fortune ended when the dispute finished, for we had no work to which to return. I did not find another job for a year, and then it was in a different colliery.

Increasingly I found myself active in union work in a voluntary capacity, and took on a quick succession of jobs – branch secretary, minimum wage agent, vice-chairman and chairman of the Bargoed Steam Coal Lodge of the South Wales Miners Federation. I was also secretary of the local section of the newly formed Labour Party, and a

Notice of injury

sub-agent in the general elections of 1922, 1923 and 1924. In 1925 I stood unsuccessfully for the post of miners' agent for the Rhymney Valley. It was a good campaign, which gave me useful experience on the public platform. The winning candidate was Bryn Roberts, later General Secretary of the National Union of Public Employees.

The mining industry was still in crisis. Unemployment was rife and many of those lucky enough to have a job only worked short-time. Early in 1926 I was sacked again because part of the mine was closed down. My trade union activities undoubtedly contributed to my dismissal.

On the 1st May 1926 when the General Strike commenced I was in London at the Kingsway Hall conference of the Miners' Federation. At one point all the miners went outside to watch the London May Day Demonstration pass. It was the most impressive sight of my life. The General Strike did not last long but the miners' dispute continued. Though none of us had any paid employment there was plenty of voluntary work for us. We developed our soup kitchens to ensure at least one meal a day for the adult population. The local authority provided for the children, but there too we played our part, serving meals and washing up. We had our evening concerts and, to raise funds for the soup kitchen, I organised a concert party involving some semi-professional artistes.

I participated in the concerts as an elocutionist because I was confident now with speaking in public. However, I vividly remember an occasion in Hengoed where I had been told of some miners blacklegging while their fellows were on strike. Perhaps I got carried away in my speech because my belt fell off and I had to conclude with one hand in my pocket tightly gripping my trousers.

* * *

The Labour College

The pioneers of the Labour College Movement recognised that the struggle against the worst evils of capitalism was more than an industrial fight; they saw clearly that the fullness of victory could only come with a wider knowledge and understanding of the workings of society. They were, in a very real sense, the enlightened missionaries of social change.

While unemployed I was taking a correspondence course in industrial history and Marxist economics, and the local miners' agent had urged me to try for the two year scholarship which the union offered at the Labour College in Earls Court London. I took the entrance exam though I had no preparation for it and to everyone's surprise (including mine) I passed.

My work with the concert parties led my friends, despite their own poverty, to help me with a decent suit and my train fare to London.

In August 1926, on my last evening in Wales, I returned home late from a dance to find the local police sergeant waiting for me. He wanted to know whether I had uttered certain seditious remarks at Hengoed about blacklegs. I confessed that I had spoken off the cuff and probably said something of the kind. He warned me that my words could get me into trouble, and he had been asked to send a full report to the Chief Constable.

When I mentioned that I was due to leave the next morning to take up my scholarship he promised to include that in his report, and I was able to leave on schedule. In my first few weeks in London I was nervous whenever a policeman walked in my direction. One Sunday, at the request of the Miners' Federation, I addressed a meeting in Battersea Park. A policeman did ask me for my name and address, but nothing ensued. As I learned afterwards, the Chief Constable had decided that no further action was needed. He hoped that some sense would be knocked into me at college, but I do not think he was aware that it was a full-time Marxist institution.

Life at the Labour College was an absorbing experience. We were removed from the day to day problems of running a trade union branch and fired with new enthusiasm. We quickly came to conclude that all the old leaders of Labour were reactionary and did not really want to overthrow capitalism. To us the revolution seemed round the corner. All we had to do was to reach for it.

We took our discussions very seriously and we were so convinced of the validity of our ideas that we seized every opportunity of passing on our knowledge to others. We rushed to accept invitations to speak at evening classes and union and Labour Party branch meetings. One such class was to have an important bearing on my career and my life. I was asked to lecture on public speaking at a class in Fulham, West London. The organiser assured me that the course would not last long, as they never did in that district. Certainly the class was small but it contained the cream of the local Labour Party, and I kept it going for more than two years until February 1928, when the Party workers in the group asked whether I would act as election agent in the LCC (London County Council) election. As a full-time student I was not supposed to undertake work of this nature but I decided to risk it. The college principal belonged to the Fulham Co-operative Men's Guild and was likely to be informed of my activities even if he did not spot my name on the election posters. Fortunately I heard nothing about it. The campaign was regarded as eminently satisfactory though we did not win the seat.

The West Fulham Labour Party decided to appoint their first full-time agent and they offered me the post. I gladly accepted, but Labour's national headquarters (Transport House) refused for a time to help with my salary, as the job had not been properly advertised. The dispute ended when Transport House asked West Fulham to release me to act as agent for an LCC by-election in Westminster (the Abbey division).

This was a fascinating experience. I took an empty house in Marsham Street and established committee rooms in New Compton Street, but very few people volunteered to help. I enlisted West Fulham's League of Youth, who thoroughly enjoyed delivering election addresses to West End clubs, hotels and business premises. Someone suggested approaching Hannen Swaffer, the former editor of the People newspaper. When I rang to ask him if he was a member of the Party, Swaffer replied with great emphasis that he had been a socialist for fifty years. I never discovered whether he actually was a member, but he was a great success at my meeting. In later years I often exploited his willingness to speak at Party demonstrations.

When I went to the count at Caxton Hall, Westminster, I expected a terrible drubbing, but we got within a thousand of the successful Tory candidate. Where the votes came from I never knew.

* * *

By-Election Honeymoon

I have already mentioned the West Fulham League of Youth. I started this group in my early days at Fulham by appealing to all the Party members to encourage their youngsters to join. One night the secretary of our Women's Section, Kate Lusher, brought to my office her daughter Norah, a slim eighteen year old with dark hair in an Eton crop. I did not like her hairstyle, and I gather she thought me a know-all. The interview did not bode well for the League of Youth, but parental pressure overcame her scruples. She agreed to be secretary, and between us we organised one of the strongest League of Youth branches in the country, with its own netball, cricket and football teams and dramatic society. As our meetings usually finished late at night I used to walk home with her. Soon we were planning walks when there were no meetings. We met during her lunch hour (she was a shorthand typist), and eventually we were seeing each other as often as we could. I suppose no one was surprised when we got engaged.

Engagement photo

Our engagement coincided with the Parliamentary Election of 1929. West Fulham had since its inception in 1918 been held by the Conservative Sir Cyril Cobb. I booked lots of halls and arranged lots of meetings, as I used to do in South Wales, but to my horror only a few people turned up. The campaign started slowly but on Election Day the Labour candidate Dr Ernest Spero defeated Cobb by more than 2000 votes.

The following January, as Norah and I were planning our wedding, Dr Spero suddenly left the country. Rumours abounded, and would have grown if we had postponed our wedding.

On the morning of my marriage (15ᵗʰ March 1930) I got up early and wandered around indoors and out, restless, impatient and nervous. I was afraid that the future might have the same insecurity and unemployment in store for us as I had known in the past. What is more, I would be responsible for my wife and later perhaps for our children.

It was a relief when the time came for me to make my way to the church of St Thomas of Canterbury in Fulham. The church was already packed with Party members. As I sat waiting for my bride, I needed a cigarette and was only prevented from reaching in my pocket by a watchful friend immediately behind me. After the ceremony we entertained our guests and in the evening we occupied a box in the Chelsea Palace variety theatre. That was the full extent of our honeymoon because the impending by-election made it inadvisable to go away.

On the 9th April Dr Spero finally resigned, leaving us to find another candidate for the by-election. We adopted a popular resident Bill Banfield, the General Secretary of the Bakers' Union. The by-election drew considerable publicity as the first test of public opinion after the Budget, which was introduced by the minority Labour Government. Then a bright journalist discovered that we had recently got married. Photographers descended on us for pictures that would be captioned 'AGENT SPENDS HONEYMOON FIGHTING BY-ELECTION'.

When the result was announced Labour held its vote. Unfortunately the Liberals had not put up a candidate this time, which helped the Conservatives regain the seat by 211 votes. The gentlemanly Bill Banfield did not ask for a recount, saying:

'In Fulham the conscientiousness of the officials ensures a fair deal, irrespective of party, and so satisfied was I that the count was correct that I made no attempt to challenge it.'

This defeat was the worst setback that I had encountered and it damaged my confidence for a while. I resigned from the agency to take up an appointment as London Organiser/Tutor for the National Council of Labour Colleges. My ambition now was to become a Parliamentary candidate. In the 1931 Election I assisted Arthur Hayday, the Labour candidate for West Nottingham, and soon afterwards the Nottingham Cooperative Society chose me as their candidate for Nottingham Central. I worked in the constituency for several years until the cost of travelling to and from my London home ended my candidature. In November 1934 I became a Labour member of the Fulham Borough Council and Chairman of the Finance Committee.

* * *

Fulham Borough Council

Local government affords the greatest satisfaction to anyone interested in public work. You move a resolution in favour of a new housing estate. You see the houses being built. You feel a sense of achievement. You have debates with your political opponents on local matters of interest to your neighbours.

I remember doing some canvassing one evening with my wife Norah, who was a candidate in a council by-election. We received the usual mixed reception from the usual assortment of householders until at one front door a big, tough looking chap said,

'Local elections, mister, you can count me out. They can get along all right without me. I'm not interested.'

I put this question to him,

'What were the first things you did this morning when you got up?'

He made the fire, he said. He had a wash. He made his wife a cup of tea, and his wife got up and prepared the breakfast. So I reminded him that it was the council officials who saw to it that the coal was not underweight and that his food was pure, and council services that provided the water and sanitation for his house.

Next they got the children off to school.

'School? That ought to make you think about local government. So much of the quality of education depends on the energy and enthusiasm of your local council.'

And so we went through his entire day. Whatever that man did, he found himself using services provided by one or other of the local councils – street lighting, libraries, fire brigades, police, parks, all sorts of welfare services, town and country planning, housing. And yet at first he said he would not bother to vote.

Fulham was building a new power station. It needed coal, which had to come up river. The previous Conservative Council had wanted to give a private shipping company the contract to deliver the coal. We took a different view. We wanted to build our own boats and to carry our own coal to our own power station. The Central Electricity Board objected to our scheme, so we sent a deputation to Sir Archibald Page the CEB Chairman. In the end we were allowed to build our own boats provided they were managed by a private company. We accepted this compromise. Some of those boats rendered distinguished service in the Second World War and we always remembered with pride our association with getting them built, not to mention our achievement in operating our own power station.

The new Labour council invited Professor Harold Laski to become an Alderman with the special task of reorganising the public libraries. For me his acceptance of the office led to a firm friendship, which lasted to his death. Harold had a remarkable personality. He loved his work for the people of Fulham. He was a loyal colleague. No task was too humble for him to undertake, and he often enlivened council proceedings with satirical speeches which discomfited the Tories and amused his colleagues and the public galleries. Yet in some ways he was a strange character. He was regarded by many as an advocate of violent revolution. He certainly challenged the assumptions of capitalist society but he believed that such a society could be transformed by public consent. He rejected the Communist conception of a proletarian dictatorship, and believed passionately in liberty. Only in a free society could men and women develop their talents and personalities to the full.

As councillors we were perturbed by the number of street accidents and by the placid acceptance of children having nowhere to play but the street. I discussed this situation with the Borough Surveyor, and asked whether the children would make more use of parks and open spaces if we appointed a Games Organiser. He investigated but was doubtful about the legality of spending public money on this. Even so we tried the idea for two months at a cost of £50. A number of people volunteered to contribute if the District Auditor imposed a surcharge. Harold Laski himself underwrote £25. However there was no surcharge. The experiment worked brilliantly and won national publicity. Some of our political foes, notably Leslie Hore-Belisha, the Minister of Transport,

Donkey race

gave us invaluable support.

For the Coronation of George VI in 1937 I was appointed chairman of the committee to plan Fulham's celebrations. As well as publishing a brochure about the borough, we organised a large fete at Hurlingham Polo Ground, which would begin with a donkey race between the mayor and me. Unfortunately the two donkeys provided were used to walking together and did not understand the concept of a race. When prodded, one would bound forward then wait for its partner. My main anxiety was to stay in the saddle during these periodic leaps especially with hundreds of children watching. The race was a dead heat, and I dismounted with relief.

* * *

Transport House 1937

As well as my unpaid work as a councillor, I was the local agent for the Whitechapel & St George's Division in East London. It was an unusual community, half Jewish, half Roman Catholic. Oswald Mosley and his fascists were trying to stir up large scale anti-Semitism. There were many conflicts, even within the Party, but everyone showed me great courtesy and consideration and helped to make my work possible. In a constituency where 13,000 had voted Labour in 1935, we built up a record membership of 3,300. I was very proud indeed to receive on the constituency's behalf the membership shield at the London Labour Party. This record has never been beaten.

My Party Chairman in Whitechapel was a dockworker, a man of enthusiasm and loyalty. Popularly known as 'Stoker' Edwards, he later became Civil Lord of the Admiralty.

I really loved my time in Whitechapel and I also enjoyed being a Fulham councillor, but in November 1937 I had to leave both offices when I successfully applied for the job of Labour Party Propaganda Officer. Friends of mine on the Party's National Executive forewarned me that I would not be appointed but I would improve my chances of getting a job at Transport House (Party Headquarters) when other vacancies occurred.

I did put my name forward but when called for interview I felt rather angry that the outcome had been predetermined. I told the committee that I was not really interested in the job in its present form. A social democratic party needed to develop educational work throughout the Labour Movement under the direction of the National Executive and not leave it to all kinds of other organisations. The committee asked many questions and I gave candid rather than diplomatic answers. Leaving the room I was convinced that I had talked myself out of the job. Indeed, I suggested to the other three candidates that the winner should entertain the others to tea. I paid for the tea.

When I took up my duties my first task was to organise speakers for a nationwide campaign called Victory for Socialism. A record number of meetings were called, though this would be equalled soon after by the Party's campaign against Neville Chamberlain's foreign policy. At this time I was collaborating with two legendary socialists Ellen Wilkinson and Stafford Cripps, both of whom were working like Trojans for the Milk for Spain fund. In December their Spain Campaign Committee organised a huge demonstration at the Albert Hall, which raised more than £3,300. There were many speakers from the Party and the trade unions, but Ellen Wilkinson's contribution was special. I believe that she and Stafford Cripps found in this campaign a satisfying outlet for their restless energy and impatience with the official machine.

I soon got to know Ernest Bevin because we were working in the same building. He was a good man to get in touch with to address a crowd. Much of my time was spent in the House of Commons, for it was always easier to get an oral invitation to speak than a written one. What a lot of meetings there were, until the declaration of War in September 1939 brought campaigning to an end. My job disappeared overnight.

Fortunately, the Government invited each of the three main parties to choose a representative to join the Ministry of Information as political consultants. My immediate chief, George Shepherd, chose me, and on the 4th September I made my way to the Ministry Headquarters in Bloomsbury to join Marjorie Maxse (Conservative) and Raymond Jones (Liberal). Sadly the political representatives were given little to do. We signed in at 9 am and out at 5 pm. Between those hours I did far less work than I had ever done before, even when I was unemployed. Occasionally, I was consulted about the personnel for the information committees being established across the nation, but I rarely had any proper work. My frustration was shared by others in the Ministry including Dick Crossman, Max Nicolson and Raymond Jones. We met informally to plan the future and we all wanted to persuade the Ministry to run a series of meetings galvanising the war effort. We even prepared some speakers' notes to show how the meetings could run. Alas, the authorities rejected the idea.

The Civil Service was paying me far more than the Labour Party had, but I was pleased to leave Bloomsbury and return to Transport House. In

February 1940 there was a by-election in London's Silvertown, and I was appointed as Labour's agent. The main parties had agreed an election truce for the duration of the War, but there were two anti-War candidates: the Communist leader Harry Polllitt and the Fascist Thomas Moran. Silvertown had been held for Labour since its inception by a popular local man Jack Jones. While he was candidate no organisation was needed. Canvassing meant Jack strolling down the streets and greeting his constituents. So I found no Party headquarters, only a few members and a candidate (James Hollins) who was not widely known.

I acquired temporary offices and planned the campaign, preparing the literature, booking the halls and arranging speakers. But our meetings flopped, while those of our opponents were packed out. The Communist Party imported hundreds of workers from all over London, who canvassed diligently and were well organised.

Four days before polling day (22nd February) I called a meeting of Party volunteers but few turned up. Allan Hodgson of the *Daily Herald* needed a story on the campaign so we drove round the constituency in his small two-seater car, looking for inspiration. Suddenly in a dockside street we came across people festooning a house with flags and bunting. Discreet inquiries revealed that the decoration was in honour of the tenant Jimmy Reynolds. He was one of the 299 British servicemen released from captivity two nights previously, when sailors from HMS Cossack boarded the German vessel Altmark. We found Jimmy and I asked if he would appear at my first big meeting in Canning Town. He not only agreed but promised to bring three mates who had also been released from the prison ship. I immediately announced this to the press.

This was a great story, not just for the *Daily Herald.* Another paper posted placards all over Silvertown stating 'Altmark Men to Speak for Labour Candidates'. The publicity drew vast crowds to the Canning Town meeting. After Philip Noel Baker's opening speech, Jimmy and his friends were introduced and as expected they received a tremendous ovation. Jimmy held up his hand for silence, and one by one they described in a natural and dignified way their experiences on the German ship. It was magnificent. Then Jimmy held up his hand again and said, 'Don't forget to vote on Thursday – Labour of course'. I realised then that I had never asked him about his politics.

My cup was full to the brim. Then Herbert Morrison made one of the best speeches I ever heard him make.

Another meeting had been arranged for the following evening. It would have been impossible to match the Altmark celebration but I decided to ask Ben Tillett, the grand old man of the Trade Union Movement, to return to the scene of his early struggles. And he ensured a packed auditorium. On arrival he went straight into the audience to shake hands with many old friends in row after row. We eventually started the meeting, exactly one hour late. But what a meeting and what a speech Ben Tillett made that night. Ellen Wilkinson, the other speaker, was right at the top of her form too.

The result – James Hollins (Labour) 14,343 votes; Harry Pollitt (Communist) 966; Thomas Moran (Fascist) 152. Labour had 92.8% of the vote.

During the by-election I had made use of the political notes that had been rejected when I was working for the Ministry of Information. One topic in particular, contrasting working conditions in democratic Britain with those in Fascist Germany, worked well as a news-sheet. A *Times* reporter spotted it and quoted it in his paper. A few days later the Ministry contacted me to ask for a copy, and I am pleased to say that it was subsequently used in overseas propaganda. By now the Ministry of Information was much better organised and doing excellent work, particularly in the overseas section.

My next post was as the Party's Regional Organiser for the Eastern Counties, which extended from Lincolnshire to East London. Many of the towns were scheduled as evacuation areas, and there was the very real threat of a German invasion. My job was to keep the Party together in the midst of war. Duplicate records were prepared and sent to Market Bosworth, to which the Party's Organisation Department had been evacuated. Local officers were advised what to do with their records if the enemy invaded.

I visited members in their homes, at work and at meetings, where attendances were inevitably small. In the autumn and winter months meetings finished early because the bombing raids started soon after dusk, and people worried about their families and their homes. But everywhere they kept the Party alive, to give such a great account of itself in the peacetime election. I am certain that if invasion had come anywhere between Grimsby and Southend, the organised members in the area would have formed the nucleus, if not the leadership, of an effective underground resistance.

My wife and children were living in a small cottage near Cropredy in Oxfordshire while I lived in a room generously put at my disposal by the Secretary of the Cambridge Labour Party. One day I was surprised to learn that inquiries were being made about me both in Cambridge and in Oxfordshire. At least six people had been interviewed and they all assured me that they had given favourable answers. Eventually I discovered from Ellen Wilkinson, who was now Under Secretary at the Ministry of Home Security, that the Government needed someone with my experience on the Regional Defence Organisation. After my spell at the Ministry of Information I had no wish to be in the Government's employ, but no one ever approached me anyway. Perhaps my six friends did not after all satisfy MI5 with their answers.

Far more to my taste was a job advertised in the New Statesman magazine for the Secretary of Labour's Research Department at Transport House, a post previously held by my good friend Arthur Greenwood. Arthur has never received the credit that he deserved for his contribution to the making of Party policy and the planning of successful Party Conferences, or for the time and energy spent in addressing meetings anywhere and at any time. I never knew his political judgement to be wrong. Now he was Minister of Reconstruction in the Coalition Government. The Research Department had been given extra responsibility by the decision of Labour's National Executive to appoint its own Central Committee of Reconstruction, with numerous sub-committees planning the social and economic transformation of the United Kingdom.

Having applied for the post I was delighted to be called for interview. The shortlisted candidates took turns to be questioned by Hugh Dalton and Harold Laski. This was an enjoyable experience, for Dalton, despite his overpowering voice and dominant personality, possessed a quick wit and an infectious sense of humour. He made an excellent chairman of an interviewing committee and always put candidates at their ease.

The competition was particularly strong, so my expectations were not high. Besides we would not know the result until the National Executive meeting weeks later. I carried on my work in the Eastern Counties, preparing myself for a letdown. Then, on the day of the vital meeting, I chanced to meet an Executive member who congratulated me on my appointment.

* * *

Research Department

Transport House, the property of the Transport & General Workers Union, is an imposing building in Smith Square Westminster, about five minutes' walk from the Houses of Parliament. The Labour Party rented office space in Transport House for the General Secretary and his staff, so that the work of the National Executive Committee and of the Party's Annual Conference could be carried out. I took up my Research Department duties in October 1941 and ran into an unexpected problem. A member of the Transport House staff wrote a letter objecting to my appointment, because I had no academic qualifications. When the Policy Committee considered the objection, Jimmy Walker MP looked round his colleagues and remarked that, if the protest was valid, only two committee members would qualify for a job at Transport House, namely Hugh Dalton and Harold Laski, the two men who made the appointment. The letter was unanimously rejected, and the writer resigned.

The Labour Party had set up a Committee of Reconstruction, with Emanuel Shinwell as Chairman and Laski as Secretary. Its role was to take evidence from 27 sub-committees, each dealing with an aspect of social and economic transformation to be achieved after the War. My Research Department had to provide the factual material for the sub-committees. As my only colleagues were five shorthand typists the work was heavy, but it was exciting too, for we were planning for the future and we were determined that the evils of the 1920s and 1930s should not be repeated.

My time with the Research Department gave me an excellent insight into the problems of policy and organisation facing the Party. Two factors also encouraged me to take a special interest in International Affairs. One was the appointment of Will Arnold Foster as my temporary assistant. He was an expert on international institutions and a strong advocate of a United Nations Organisation for collective security. He had joyously welcomed the publication of the Atlantic Charter in August 1941 and spent hours each day preparing a detailed interpretation – far too detailed and premature for us to publish. He came to my office daily to discuss the latest additions and amendments to his document. These conversations were both exciting and educational, and later proved of immense help to me.

The second factor was the decision to hold a joint meeting of the Policy Committee, of which I was secretary, and the International Sub-committee. There I learned of Harold Laski's dream of a single Socialist International Organisation able to combine the socialist forces of Europe. He believed that the Russian workers would play a full part. There were many exiled social democrats in London, and generally they did not share Laski's optimism. They were profoundly sceptical about any overtures to Stalin on this issue. The 1942 Labour Conference decided to send a delegation to Russia as soon as practicable, because 'the future of the whole of civilisation depends upon the establishment of a permanent basis of friendship with the Soviet Union'. The delegation could not be sent until 1946.

The Research Department had a good deal of day-to-day work, briefing local councillors and others to help them understand White Papers, Defence Regulations and the like. With the encouragement of the Party Secretary Jim Middleton, I started a monthly bulletin (priced one penny) explaining the new regulations. This proved a success. I also worked with the National Council of Labour and the National Union of Mineworkers to prepare a scheme for Government control of the mining industry after the War. In conjunction with another sub-committee, chaired by Durham Miners' leader Sam Watson, we prepared plans for the public ownership of coal, gas and electricity for submission to the 1944 Labour Conference. Little more than two years later a Labour Government started to implement this policy. It must have given particular pride and satisfaction to Manny Shinwell, the Chairman of the Central Reconstruction Committee, to pilot these measures onto the Statute Book.

The early 1940s were an altogether fruitful period for the publication of policy documents, all of which were submitted to and approved by Annual Conferences. Probably the best written was 'Wings for Peace', which recommended the post-war creation of a World Air Authority owning and operating the main air routes around the world. In Europe all airways, domestic as well as international, would be operated by Europa under licence from the World Aviation Authority. The author was Will Arnold Foster. Each day he had come into my room to discuss his views and read me his additions to the document, many of them too premature and far too detailed for publication.

The most controversial document was on the reform of local government. It sought to introduce area and regional authorities with specific functions. I believed that this dual structure could meet the needs of post-war Britain while preserving the democratic character of local government. I addressed conferences of Labour councillors throughout England, Scotland and Wales. Many were persuaded but the opposition was still very powerful. Eventually the issue came before the Annual Conference at the Central Hall Westminster in June 1943. The Party's National Executive backed the scheme, though in fairness to Herbert Morrison I must point out that he opposed it from the start. I was chosen by the National Executive to wind up the debate on its behalf, the first time that a staff member from Transport House had received such an opportunity. A card vote was called, which showed 1,542,000 votes in favour, and 966,000 against. Because of the substantial opposition the scheme was dropped. I regret this, for it could have created direct democratic control of local health services and paved the way for a greater measure of devolution of democratic authority. We are left with the anomalies, untidiness and weakness of our present structure.

* * *

Labour Party Secretary

The Secretary of the British Labour Party is the senior administrative and executive officer of the Party outside Parliament. He is responsible for the running of Head Office and for nationwide organisation. He liaises closely with Party leaders and with the Parliamentary Labour Party, whose paid staff are under his supervision. He acts as secretary to the Party's National Executive Committee and is intimately associated with the formation of Party policy. Finally, he is 'authorised to make public

Morgan with Jim Middleton

statements from time to time, as required by circumstances, in harmony with the declared policy of the Party'. Working under him are the National Agent and the Chief Woman Officer, and the Secretaries of the International, Press, Research and Finance Departments. In the 1940s the Secretary had a staff of around eighty people, who occupied thirty-six offices scattered on almost every floor of the seven storey Transport House. In addition, there were thirty or more full-timers attached to regional headquarters throughout the country, and some two hundred and forty salaried agents.

The Secretary is appointed by the Party's Annual Conference but is not subject to re-election. Ramsay Macdonald was the first Secretary from 1900 to 1911, though the office did not appear in the Constitution until 1903. He was succeeded by Arthur Henderson, who held the office until 1934. Both men were Members of Parliament; the 1918 Constitution laid it down that the Secretary 'shall devote his whole time to the work of the Party, but this shall not prevent him from being a candidate for or a Member of Parliament'. In 1934 when Jim Middleton succeeded Arthur Henderson the Constitution was changed to bar the Secretary from being an MP.

Jim Middleton had been working for the Party since 1903. When I served under him at Transport House I always found him helpful, encouraging and ready to give me the freedom to try anything that might be beneficial to the Party. He had been Ramsay Macdonald's assistant in the days when the Party was run from a back bedroom in Macdonald's London flat. Jim was subsequently Assistant Secretary to Arthur Henderson, and carried the bulk of administrative work while Henderson was Britain's Foreign Secretary (hence the Constitutional change of 1934). Labour has never had a more faithful, loyal and sincere servant than Jim Middleton. He was very close to Ramsay Macdonald, whose children he had nursed when they worked together in the formative years of the Party. Macdonald's defection from Labour in 1931 was a bitter blow, but Jim never forgot his friend's earlier contribution to British socialism.

In March 1942 Middleton reached his 65th birthday, the retiring age for all Party officials. The Executive extended his stay but this did not prevent considerable speculation about his possible successor. Most political observers decided well in advance that the post would be filled by my friend Maurice Webb, the Parliamentary Correspondent of the *Daily Herald.* I took little more than academic interest in the predictions because I never envisaged applying for the post. I was more interested to hear that Scott Lindsay, Secretary of the Parliamentary Labour Party, was also about to retire.

The Chairman of Labour's National Executive that year was George Ridley MP, a great friend of mine. We spent many pleasant hours in his Ealing home, in his Clay Cross constituency and at meetings and conferences all over the country. One day he surprised me by asking whether I would be interested in the post of Party Secretary. Then I received a letter from Harold Laski urging me to be Jim Middleton's successor. I was having a drink with Bill Robinson of the Shop, Distributive and Allied Workers Union, when we were joined by a journalist who claimed to have come from a luncheon party at the Howard Hotel. He said to me, 'You'll never be the secretary of the Labour Party.' Apparently the successor to Jim Middleton had been discussed by National Executive members at the lunch, who reckoned that Maurice Webb already had enough votes to win – eleven votes out of twenty four. This really annoyed Bill Robinson, who felt that his vote was being taken for granted. He turned to me and asked if I would run against Maurice Webb and if I gave my word whether I would stick by it. I assured him on both points. Other trade union members of the Executive later added their support including Sam Watson (Durham Miners), Fred Burrows (National Union of Railwaymen), and George Dallas (Transport and General).

To my great sorrow George Ridley passed away early in 1944. Many of his constituents urged me to be the Labour candidate in the by-election. It was the sort of division that aspiring politicians dream of, because George had won by over 16,000 votes. I declined their invitation because my ambition was now to be Party Secretary.

With Jim Middleton approaching his 67th birthday, the search for his successor got under way. The National Executive decided by a narrow majority to retain the ban on the Secretary being also a Member of Parliament. On the 22nd March 1944 I and five other shortlisted candidates were interviewed by the National Executive. I had lunch with two Executive members, who prepared me for defeat. When the selection meeting began I stayed in my own room on the fifth floor and carried on working until I was summoned. I then answered the questions put to me and returned to my office, only to be asked to return to the Executive meeting, where I was welcomed as the prospective Secretary of the Labour Party. By this time it was 4 pm, and there was little that I could do as I was due to start fire-watching with Arthur Deakin, which would last all night. So I celebrated my appointment protecting Transport

House, the building over which I was to preside.

My appointment was confirmed at the Annual Conference in October 1944 and on the 5th July 1945 the British electors voted for Labour's first ever majority government.

* * *

Ernest Bevin

On the 26th July 1945, now knowing that the Conservatives had lost the 1945 General Election, Clem Attlee arrived at Transport House. He was not a man for long flowery speeches, and there was really very little to say because we all felt the same: overwhelmed. Even Attlee was as near to being overwhelmed as I ever saw him. 'Very good, isn't it, Morgan?' was all he said.

He wanted a private meeting with Ernest Bevin and Herbert Morrison. It was impossible to use my room because so many people had crowded in, so we went up to Ernest Bevin's office. I was also in attendance because the Secretary has the duty and the privilege of advising the Party Leader on organisation, and on foreign and domestic policy. At the meeting I learned more about the campaign to empower the new Parliamentary Labour Party to elect its leader, who would thus become Prime Minister. I was unaware that Herbert Morrison had sent telegrams to Stafford Cripps and others, urging them to press this view on Clem Attlee.

Attlee began the meeting by discussing the formation of a government. Morrison demanded that nothing be done until the Parliamentary Labour Party had met and elected its leader; this was customary practice at the start of each Parliament. He told us that many in the Party supported his view and during the meeting he received a phone call from Stafford Cripps, who, according to Morrison, took the same line.

Of course Attlee disagreed, as did Ernest Bevin and I. Ernest felt that Labour would lose the public's good will if it appeared to hesitate about taking over the government.

At 3.30 the letter arrived from Churchill conceding defeat. Morrison instantly repeated his demand for a meeting of the Parliamentary Party. It would have taken two days to gather the successful candidates from all over the United Kingdom. Attlee, Bevin and I believed it would be fatal to delay accepting the Royal Command for three days. It was decided that Attlee should go to the Palace as soon as the invitation arrived. Meanwhile, I arranged the meeting of the Parliamentary Labour Party.

Strictly speaking Morrison's suggestion was correct. Furthermore, he honestly regarded himself as more suited than Attlee to lead the Party. If we had not gained so fantastic a victory, he might well have had his chance.

With that important decision made, our discussions became more general. Bevin turned to Attlee and remarked, 'Well, Clem, I don't know what you would like me to do. I could stick to the Ministry of Labour, but its plan for demobilisation and the transfer of men to peacetime jobs has been completed. It is now merely a matter of administration. I could go to the Board of Trade, where my long years of contact and negotiation with British employers might be of some value. As you know, however, my special hobby for some years has been taxation.'

Attlee's only reply was in the form of a question, 'Who would you make Foreign Secretary?' to which Bevin answered without hesitation 'Hugh Dalton'. This was the only reference to the matter during the meeting. Attlee and I left the room together, and as we walked along the corridor I ventured the opinion that Bevin's speech on Foreign Affairs at the recent Party Annual Conference had enabled him to walk straight into the Foreign Office. Attlee's reply was typically brief:

'Of course it did.'

Since then the story has arisen that Hugh Dalton was Foreign Secretary for six hours until King George intervened. John Wheeler-Bennett, in the official biography *King George VI: His Life and Reign* (Macmillan 1958), quoted from the Royal Archives to show that when Attlee intended to make Dalton Foreign Secretary, 'His Majesty begged him to think carefully about this and suggested Mr Bevin would be a better choice'. In an interview for the Observer newspaper (23rd August 1959) Clem Attlee stated, 'When I saw the King I had not come to a definite conclusion... I don't recollect that the King expressed any strong views on the subject, but he seemed inclined to prefer Mr Bevin as Foreign Secretary.'

At 7.30 pm on the 26th July 1945, the Party held a victory rally in Central Hall Westminster. Attlee was at the Palace accepting the Royal Invitation to form a government. At the rally, Bevin asked me what office he was likely to be offered. He hoped to know soon, as he and his wife were about to leave for a holiday in Cornwall. I warned him that the holiday would be postponed and he would be accompanying Attlee to Potsdam. This took him by surprise, and frankly I do not think he believed me, but he did indeed travel to Potsdam as I had predicted. Attlee's judgment was sound, and gave Great Britain one of its best Foreign Secretaries.

Bevin's major achievement was to secure Marshall Aid in 1947, which saved many countries from starvation and chaos. He knew how to put Marshall's ideas into practice. America was the only country capable of supplying the goods that we and other European nations needed so badly. Ernest Bevin seized upon Mr Marshall's Harvard speech, and took the initiative in bringing together the countries of Europe to form the Organisation for European Economic Co-operation, hoping that together they could plan a recovery programme. He was frustrated by the Soviet Union's refusal to allow Eastern Europe to participate. It became necessary to create the North Atlantic Treaty Organisation because of Russia's encroachment in Europe. Bevin's part in the formation of NATO was amply justified by subsequent events.

This did not stop him from becoming impatient with American politicians and government. I well remember his bitterness over the outcome of the Anglo-American Commission in Palestine. He thought he had a solution to the Palestinian problem. Because there was a state election in New York, President Truman refused to support any proposal that might upset the Jewish lobby. Here was a dream shattered as far as Bevin was concerned.

Ernest's loyalty to Clem Attlee could not be questioned. On one occasion some Cabinet colleagues came to his office, urging him to replace Attlee as Prime Minister with their assistance. He told me this at once and finished by saying, 'It's Attlee's turn today and if I joined in this game it would be my turn tomorrow.'

Ernest Bevin never forgot his Transport & General Workers Union. He kept his office in Transport House, and a lot of work was still being done for him by his former private secretary, Ivy Saunders. He was always round the building and no member of staff, his or ours, was too humble for him to stop and talk to.

We got on very well indeed. He would just push his head in my door, come in, take a seat, and start talking; about his job, his intentions, what he was trying to achieve and the difficulties that he encountered. Then he often asked me to see him at the Foreign Office, because Socialist parties were playing a powerful part in Europe at the time.

If you met any ambassadors or officers who worked with him you would find tremendous admiration. His staff spoke of him not merely with respect, but with pure affection. They knew that he recognised their loyalty and supported them if they made a mistake. He gave scope for young people to express their views freely, and he never held it against anyone whose ideas differed from his own.

Ernest Bevin was one of nature's gentlemen and he never lost the common touch.

* * *

Labour in Government

Having chosen Ernest Bevin as Foreign Secretary, Clem Attlee quickly set the machinery of government in action. He invited Herbert Morrison to Downing Street and offered him the office of Lord President of the Council. William Whiteley, the new Government Chief Whip, sat in on the discussion and told me about it afterwards. Apparently Herbert was not at all impressed, so when Attlee left the room to take a phone call, Whiteley pointed out that by becoming Lord President Morrison would effectively be Number 2 in the Government. When Attlee returned, Morrison accepted the position.

He was in many ways the ideal choice with his wide experience. He had previously served as Minister of Transport, Leader of the London County Council and Secretary of the London Labour Party. For many years he had been active in policy making and he was Chairman of the Campaign Committee for the 1945 General Election.

There was one disturbing issue left over from the Election. Harold Laski was the kind of speaker who could paint a beautiful pattern, an enlarged vista that would lead to sudden generalisations. This habit could sometimes be exploited. On Monday 18th June 1945 the *Nottingham Guardian* had published a letter from Mr HCC Carlton, of which I quote the first paragraph:

'Attending a meeting in the Newark Market Place on Saturday night I was horrified to hear Professor Harold J Laski, Chairman of the Socialist Party, when enumerating reforms he wanted to see, declare, "If we cannot have them by fair means we shall use violence to obtain them". A member of the audience immediately challenged him and said, "You are inviting revolution from the platform". Prof Laski replied, "If we cannot get reforms we desire we shall not hesitate to use violence even if it means revolution".'

Air Vice-Marshall Champion de Crespigny, the Labour candidate, who shared the platform with Laski, wrote to the *Nottingham Guardian* denying that the professor made any such statement; he himself had repeatedly made it plain that he stood for constitutional government and democratic methods.

Laski issued the following statement:

'My answer at the meeting was entirely different. What I said was, it was very much better to make changes in time of war when men were ready for great changes and willing to make them by consent through the urgency of war than to wait for the urgency to disappear through victory, and then to find that there was no consent to change what the workers felt an intolerable burden. That was the way that a society drifted to violence. We had it in our power to do by consent that which in other nations had been done by violence.'

He warned that he would issue a writ for libel against Mr Carlton and against anyone who published the letter. Nevertheless the *Daily Express* and the *London Evening Standard* both reprinted the letter, so Laski issued writs against both papers as well as the *Nottingham Guardian*. He also acted against the *Newark Advertiser*, on the basis of its report of the meeting. This was due to be heard by the Lord Chief Justice on the 26th November. The other newspapers reasoned that the result of that case would indicate how they would fare when their actions were heard, so the *Daily Express* provided the defence for the *Newark Advertiser*.

Laski had consulted lawyers and was acting independently though as a friend I was kept informed. The press had painted a picture of a tough, hard-left Marxist whereas he was a kindly man who worried if he felt he had offended anyone. He went on public platforms to explain his beliefs but none of the explanations were given anything like the same degree of publicity. He took the legal action in the interests of the Party. I thought he had a very good case, but after four days in court the jury decided that the report was fair and accurate. Judgment was given for the defendants with costs.

I was with Clem Attlee at 10 Downing Street when the result came through on the tape. My mind turned to the financial consequences for Harold Laski. He owned the house in which he lived and he possessed a valuable library of 10,000 volumes, the pride of his life. I knew also of the insurance policy provided by the London School of Economics, but I felt sure that he could not meet the legal costs without selling his home and book collection. Even then he could face bankruptcy.

I told Attlee of my fears and asked if he would object to my launching an unofficial fund to assist Laski. The Leader could well have objected to the Party Secretary raising an unofficial fund, but he was happy for me to proceed. Indeed, he made a private donation. I then contacted Jim Griffiths, the Party Chairman, who without hesitation approved my decision.

A heart-warming response came from people in all walks of life, at home and overseas. From the USA I received $7,453. The final total was

£14,290, which paid all of Laski's costs and left a surplus of £2,370. Through the medium of the press, I offered to refund some or all of the money to any subscriber who wished to contact me. Only one person did and I returned the £25 donation in full. The rest of the money was used to institute scholarships in Laski's name.

It is striking how popular you become when your party is in government. Someone from a well-known legal family asked to see me 'on a very important and confidential matter'. Apparently he had been in the Civil Service during the war and felt that he had been unjustly left off the Honours List. He was ready to give the Labour Party £5000 to rectify this injustice. Then a wealthy businessman told me that he wanted to be a Labour MP. He even named the constituency, where Labour had a majority of over 20,000. I pointed out that the constituency already had a Labour MP. He replied, 'Oh but we can pension him off', obviously intending to provide the necessary money to achieve this. It occurred to me to ask whether he was a Party member.

'Oh no', he replied, 'but I'm willing to join.' I am afraid that ended the interview very abruptly.

Nor was the fact that Labour was in government lost on the Communist Party of Great Britain. At our Annual Conference in 1946 they made their seventh application for affiliation to the Labour Party. As in other countries, the Communists were trying to compensate for their failure in free elections by becoming a fifth column within a more successful democratic party. Had they been granted affiliation in Britain, they would have introduced bitter sectarian quarrels into every Labour Party branch in the country. Our National Executive wanted to obviate once and for all these stale, futile arguments with people with whom we have so little in common, so we proposed an amendment to our constitution to ensure this. The amendment barred affiliation with all parties not already affiliated which had 'their own programme, principles and policy for distinctive and separate propaganda, or possessing branches in the constituencies, or engaged in the promotion of Parliamentary or local government candidatures, or owing allegiance to any political organisation situated abroad'. I wound up the debate on behalf of the National Executive. Many in the Party, indeed in the Government, doubted whether the Conference would approve this amendment with its momentous implications, but as I anticipated the Conference gave overwhelming support.

Historians have without exception overlooked the importance of this amendment. It meant that the Labour Conference would no longer have to endure the Communists' demand every three years and could devote its time to more important matters instead of having to hear the same old dreary arguments. Their hopes of affiliation to Labour destroyed, the Communists intensified their efforts to infiltrate the unions and the Co-operative Movement. In September 1947, the Soviet Union created the Cominform to co-ordinate the activities of Communist Parties across the globe. Speaking at Bristol on the 9th October, I discussed the consequences of this:

> 'There's a new cold war on. It is a war against European socialism and it has been launched by the Russians and eight other European Communist Parties... The world consequences of this new Communist move may yet be momentous. Its immediate consequences for European socialism can clearly be seen. The Communist honeymoon with European socialism is over.'

Sure enough the British Communists began a prolonged smear campaign against the Government. They called on their supporters to 'fight for a new Labour Government based on the forces of the Left and more progressive sections of the Labour Movement'. The National Executive gave me a free hand to counter this campaign, and in the columns of the *Daily Herald* and elsewhere I answered point by point the arguments of Harry Pollitt, the Communists' leader, and of his adherents. My argument was simple: 'The Labour Party believes in Parliamentary democracy and in a free society in which all citizens can play their part in controlling the nation's political and economic destinies. To the Labour Party no form of society would be acceptable from which individual liberty and toleration were absent.' I called on all Party members to be on their guard against Communist activity in their trade unions. A resolution at the 1948 Annual Conference challenging my circular was overwhelmingly defeated.

Of course the Communists never ceased trying to disrupt the Labour Movement. Their successes were few, though apathy did allow them excessive influence within some trade unions. For the most part British socialists have not been tempted by the 'kiss of death', as I once termed Communist pleas for unity. In November 1952, Harry Pollitt wrote an article for the *Daily Worker* entitled 'TWO WORDS MAKE MR PHILLIPS SHUDDER'. The two words were unity and peace. Harry was right; I have often shuddered at the crimes committed by the Communists in the name of unity and peace.

Any fair-minded assessment of the post-war Labour Government should concede that the successes in dealing with the multitude of political and economic problems far outweigh the failures and disappointments. The minimum requirements that we set ourselves were the attainment of full employment; the redistribution of resources so that people were protected against economic insecurity; a great housing drive; and the maximum opportunities provided by the Education Act of 1944 so that our cultural heritage should be denied to none.

After the 1945 Election things went well for a time. It cannot be said that conditions in Britain offered ideal prospects for a Labour Government. We were still fighting the last battles of a most destructive war, and the vast majority of the manpower needed for socialist reconstruction was either engaged in the war or making equipment for the war. The world shortage of food caused particular difficulties for Britain, but rationing and price controls ensured fair distribution and prevented the runaway inflation experienced by most other countries. Generally people understood the difficulties and gave us encouraging support in the local elections of 1945 and 1946. At the height of the fuel crisis in February 1947, the working people of Normanton in Yorkshire walked through a snowstorm to give the Labour candidate an overwhelming victory, and the Conservative vote actually fell. Between 1945 and the end of 1947 Labour lost no seat in a by-election that it had secured in the General Election. It was the first Government in the 20th Century of which this could be said.

Lease-lend had finished, and the Government had to negotiate loans from the USA and Canada to keep things going. We did not draw full benefit from these because of the rapid rise in prices in the United States. Yet Labour was able to carry out its mandate of nationalising the railways, the Bank of England, cable and wireless communication, and the coal industry. The Trades Dispute Act of 1927 was repealed, and preparations were made for a National Health Service. Had Labour not been in office, the post-war period would have been marked by industrial upheaval and unrest, with strikes and lockouts paralysing the economy. Nothing of the kind occurred, and the time lost through industrial disputes was negligible compared with what happened after the 1914-18 war.

In 1947 the nation's coal stocks, already at a low level, faced great demands during an unusually severe winter, and could not be replenished because the atrocious weather hindered road and rail transport, and prevented coal ships from sailing round the coast. The fuel shortage, which necessitated drastic cuts in the amount of gas, electricity, and coal available to industry and to domestic consumers, was no-one's fault, but it set many people against the Labour Government.

Yet, when in all our history have so many vast and radical changes been packed into the first three years of government? Five great Acts (National Insurance, Health Service, Industrial Injuries, National Assistance and the Children's Act), together with the Family Allowances Act, started by the coalition and implemented by Labour, changed the outlook of every British citizen – from fear of the future to confidence in a basic minimum living standard, with provision for family and dependants. As the 1920s (two million unemployed) and the 1930s (savage cuts in benefits, 200,000 houses unfit for habitation) passed into history, I gave this advice at a meeting in Peckham, London:

> 'To those younger members of this audience who do not remember what Toryism really means I would say, "Ask your Dad". He can confirm the truth from his own experience.'

I was proud to celebrate the Government's achievements, though I did suffer an embarrassing episode in 1949. We had issued a four-page leaflet headed 'What Does This Picture Mean?' It showed an unemployed man who chained himself to the railings of the Labour Exchange in 1938. Page two gave the answer: 'It means there were always between one and two million unemployed in 18 years of Tory rule.'

The third page, headed New Britain Newsreel, contained four photographs, one of which showed a curly-haired baby in a pram. The caption read: 'The prams of Britain are filled with the bonniest babies in living memory. Britain today gives mother and children a better chance of good health than anywhere else in the world.' Infant mortality was at its lowest ever and children were 'taller, heavier and healthier than ever before'. The photograph of the baby was chosen from a collection of 13 supplied by a picture library in response to our request for suitable photographs of post-war babies. A woman in Southwark, who collected royal pictures, thought that she recognised this particular baby. Turning the pages of her scrapbook she found the same picture cut from a 1936 *Daily Express.* It showed Prince Edward, later the Duke of Kent. We hastily withdrew the leaflet.

By 1950 food was more plentiful, a number of controls had been relaxed, and more than a million extra homes had been provided. Our affiliated membership was over five million, a Party record. When the General Election came on the 23rd February 1950 the margins were tight. *Time Magazine* (6th March 1950) describes how my feelings changed hour by hour as the results came in. Apparently I was 'feverishly scribbling calculations on bits of blue paper. One Labourite looked at the news ticker, whispered "We're down to 14!" Everyone heard him. The ticker throbbed on. Phillips's ashtray overflowed. He sat back silent, jaw in hand; then he got up, glanced out of the window, sat down again and lighted another cigarette.'

In the end we were victorious and we increased our total vote (the turnout was a remarkable 83.9%), but the Government's majority fell to just five seats.

The election had caused us to postpone until July our celebration of the 50th Anniversary of the Labour Party's formation. As I said at a Labour Party fete in Glastonbury,

> 'The 129 delegates who gathered at the Memorial Hall in February 1900 attracted little attention at the time... But the decision which they took at that meeting has led to a revolution in the lives of ordinary folk throughout the length and breadth of Britain.'

Unfortunately, five difficult years of government had taken their toll. Ill health forced Stafford Cripps to resign as Chancellor of the Exchequer in October 1950, and Ernest Bevin left the Foreign Office the following February. Both men died soon afterwards. Prime Minister Attlee himself had to enter hospital over Easter 1951 at a particularly difficult time.

Our participation in the Korean War placed a heavy burden on the UK's economy. The continued scramble for raw materials accelerated the price of imported goods and the cost of living rose sharply. In the 1951 Budget Hugh Gaitskell, the new Chancellor, imposed charges for the first time on the supply of dentures and spectacles under the National Health Service. This caused the resignation of Nye Bevan (Minister of Labour), Harold Wilson (President of the Board of Trade) and John Freeman (Parliamentary Secretary to the Ministry of Supply), who all objected to the charges on principle.

In the middle of August 1951 Clem Attlee invited me to a private meeting in the House of Commons attended by, among others, Herbert Morrison, (James) Chuter Ede (Leader of the House) and the Chief Whip William Whiteley. Attlee wanted our advice on whether to hold a General Election in the near future. Morrison and I strongly opposed the idea. We felt the Party needed far more time to prepare itself, but the majority disagreed with us. I asked Attlee what I should do about the Annual Conference, scheduled for the first week in October. He advised me to proceed with the normal arrangements. I did this while discreetly preparing for the election.

On Wednesday the 19th September I received a hand written note from Attlee saying that any further delay in announcing the election date would only benefit the Tories. Consequently he would make an announcement on Friday the 21st, the morning after a Conservative political broadcast. However, within a few hours something caused a change of mind, for he sent me a second note, which informed me in his laconic style that he would announce the Election date on the 9 o'clock news that same evening. Two days later Nye Bevan, Jennie Lee and Harold Wilson put out a pamphlet ('Going My Way') attacking Hugh Gaitskell's Budget and the Party's defence policy. The Conservatives were quick to exploit a 'split' in the Labour Party and hoped to frighten voters with the prospect of Nye Bevan as Prime Minister.

As polling would take place on the 25th October, a full Party Conference was out of the question. The National Executive decided on a two-and-a-half-day Conference with one item on the agenda, the Election Manifesto, which would be prepared by Nye Bevan, Hugh Dalton, Sam Watson and myself. The Conference did begin with a private session, where I gave details of the election services that we were making available. There was a long discussion and I promised to take into account the many suggestions made by delegates. The Conference was an enthusiastic one, and the participants went away determined to secure a third Labour victory.

Sadly, as Morrison and I had feared, the election came too soon. The Conservatives scraped home with a majority of 17, though our total vote increased once more. Had we waited a bit longer we, not the Tories, would have benefitted from the fall in price of raw materials.

* * *

Nye Bevan

In the early 1950s the Labour Party was bedevilled by arguments over whether the West should rearm Germany. At an international socialist gathering in Paris in October 1950, I made it clear that no decision had been taken:

> 'If the Soviet Union can be persuaded to change her policy without German rearmament or if rearmament risks provoking a war for German unity, then we must not rearm Germany'.

The Foreign Office publicly repudiated my statement because the Government had agreed in New York that 'Germany should be enabled to make an appropriate contribution to the build-up of the defence of Western Europe', but in my experience most Party members were still opposed to the idea. Indeed a year and a half later, when Labour's National Executive discussed the issue with French and German socialists, opinion even within the British delegation was divided. Barbara Castle opposed rearmament fearing it would increase East-West tension. Hugh Dalton and Mark Hewitson felt that the Germans could not be trusted with arms. Despite misgivings, Wilfred Burke and I now believed rearmament inevitable as the Russians had not changed their attitude.

One of the leading participants in the dispute was Nye Bevan. I had known him in Wales in the 1920s and we had kept in touch ever since. We were always the best of friends although you might not have guessed it from the exchange of insults that characterised our conversations. I remember an occasion in 1950 when he and I attended a lunch at the Yugoslav Embassy. Nye told me privately that he had written a letter to Attlee announcing his resignation from the Government but he could not decide whether to post it. After the lunch he invited me back to his Cliveden Place house and there we sat talking until nearly 3 am. Then Nye still wearing his slippers drove me back to Fulham and came with me into my house. My wife Norah awoke and joined us. The discussion continued but the letter was never sent.

The General Election of 1950 left the Labour Government with a majority of only five. Hugh Gaitskell, Labour's Chancellor, announced a Budget on the 10th April 1951 which contained tax increases and, for the first time, charges on National Health glasses and dentures. Nye Bevan resigned as Minister of Labour, and the problem of the Labour Government became the problem of the Labour Party. On the 25th April the Party's National Executive issued a statement approving Gaitskell's Budget, supporting the defence programme as a necessary contribution to collective security and calling on all members to stand firmly behind the Labour Government. The following day I received a joint letter from Nye Bevan, Barbara Castle, Tom Driberg and Ian Mikardo protesting that the Executive was taking sides in the controversy. I wrote back:

> 'No-one will dispute your statement that the National Executive Committee and the Government must preserve their separate identities and that the NEC has no obligation automatically to endorse Government policy. This fact itself however leaves the NEC free to comment on the work and policies of any Government – Labour no less than Tory.'

Both letters were republished in the NEC's report but the matter was not raised at the subsequent 1951 Annual Conference.

I had been asked to prepare a 4,000-word statement on Party policy for the Conference and I naturally included the re-armament programme and its effect on the country's economy. When I presented the statement to the National Executive on the 25th July, Nye and his three colleagues argued against the paragraphs relating to defence. The rest of the Executive Committee approved the whole document and it was published a month later as 'Our First Duty – Peace'. Inevitably when I launched it at a press conference the journalists asked whether it was an election manifesto or a direct answer to Nye and his supporters (already dubbed the Bevanites). My reply in each case was a firm no. The Prime Minister had told me a few days before that he favoured an Election in the near future but no decision had been reached. And the pamphlet was intended to clarify the Government's policy for the general public rather than to answer the Bevanite view point by point.

As I mentioned in the previous chapter, when Attlee did announce the Election date, we had to alter the Conference arrangements and prepare a manifesto, with the result that 'Our First Duty – Peace' never got debated. The Executive delegated the drafting of the manifesto to Nye Bevan, Hugh Dalton, Sam Watson and me. I sent each of my colleagues a first draft, inviting them to suggest amendments and additions. We met at Scarborough on the Friday before the Conference to thrash out an agreement. Our proposed manifesto was approved by the National Executive on Sunday, and printed the same evening so that it could be issued to the delegates and the press the following morning.

The Right and Left of the Party had called a truce during the Election campaign, though several trade union leaders were still smarting from an attack in the Bevanite pamphlet 'Going Our Way'. After a National Executive meeting on the 24th September I was able to tell the press that 'there was no difficulty, no row and no fight which would benefit the headlines.' The Left even agreed to cancel a rally at Scarborough, which had been timed to clash with an official demonstration.

The Conference followed the usual pre-election pattern. After I had given an update on the campaign and the arrangements for the election, the delegates debated the manifesto. Faced with the real enemy, the Conservatives, the Labour Party was united and intent on victory. During the campaign morale was good. Despite my reservations about the choice of date, and despite the redistribution of seats, the Labour Government had recently put into effect, victory seemed possible. Instead, the 1951 election was the beginning of eight lean years in which personal squabbling increased, and the prospect of a united and victorious Labour Party diminished.

At the very first National Executive meeting after the election, the union leaders took their revenge on Nye for 'Going Our Way'. The old wounds were reopened, to the delight of the press.

I presented at the same meeting a detailed report on our election campaign and outlined the tasks to be undertaken to ensure victory next time: a recruiting campaign for individual members; a build-up of funds at local and national level; the appointment of more full-time election agents; and the intensification of educational and propaganda activities. As 1951 came to a close, we put my plans into effect. Over the next twelve months we recruited 138,249 members, more than making up for the 31,000 that we lost after the 1950 Election, and we fared well in the local elections. We also produced a series of discussion documents and informative pamphlets.

The dispute over re-armament dragged on. In March 1952 Nye Bevan and 56 other Labour MPs voted against the Conservative Government's White Paper even though they had been advised to abstain. I was anxious to avoid a serious clash at the Party's Annual Conference because the arguments were already affecting the rank and file members. My suggestion was that the Conference should discuss general statements of policy which had been published in advance and discussed at local branch level. This led to three documents – 'Facing the Facts' (An Interim statement on Home Policy); 'Towards World Plenty'; and 'The Problems of Foreign Policy'. I wanted, as *The Economist* magazine noted (12 April 1952), to transform 'the Party's Annual Conference from the battleground that it had become into the forum that it used to be and ought to be again'. Unfortunately I was being over optimistic. For the foreign policy debate we received 43 resolutions backing the Bevanite line of a reduction in the arms programme.

The newspapers expected a showdown. They were to be disappointed but I still regard the 1952 Conference at Morecombe as the worst that I have ever attended. The size of the hall permitted visitors to outnumber delegates, a situation exploited by left-wingers and Communists. There were constant boos and interruptions, Hugh Dalton and Herbert Morrison lost their National Executive places to Harold Wilson and Dick Crossman, and Arthur Deakin used his fraternal delegate speech to launch a fierce attack on *Tribune*, the Bevanite magazine.

'Facing the Facts' received almost unanimous approval, but there were serious divisions in the re-armament debate. Walter Padley's motion calling for the arms bill to be reduced was only narrowly defeated, and many of the speeches were bitter. The press seized on every unpleasant incident, and people inside and outside our movement overlooked the vast amount of agreement shown at Conference. Only the dissensions and the bitterness were remembered.

At a meeting in Stalybridge two days after Conference, Hugh Gaitskell deplored 'the number of resolutions and speeches which were Communist-inspired, based not even on *Tribune* so much as on the *Daily Worker*'. He urged the Party's National Executive to deal with Communist infiltration. However, in the hope of patching up the internal quarrels, I wrote an article for the Labour magazine *Fact* entitled 'The Truth About The Split'. I referred to far worse splits in the Party's history and pointed out the many issues on which Right and Left were united:

> 'There has never been a time in our Party's history when Communist influence has been so weak.'

At its next meeting the National Executive discussed Gaitskell's speech (he was not a member of the Committee at that time) and someone mentioned my article. A week or two later I was astonished to receive press cuttings from the *Edinburgh Evening News* and two regional papers describing a non-existent vote of censure on me for my article in *Fact*. The cuttings even gave details of the vote, though it never happened. With the Executive's backing I instituted legal proceedings, and on the 4th March 1953 the newspapers agreed to pay me full damages and costs, and to publish a prominent and detailed rebuttal of the story.

With the public perception of a divided party we failed to make progress in the by-elections. In November 1952 at Wycombe, one of their marginal seats, the Conservatives actually increased their majority. This could have had unpleasant consequences for me. In the radio programme 'Any Questions', broadcast a year previously, I had remarked that if the Government's majority was not reduced within a year I would eat my hat. While I was pondering which headpiece would be most easily digested, Winston Churchill, speaking in the House of Commons, absolved me from my promise:

> 'I do not think such an unpalatable ordeal is needed with the approach of the Christmas season. I have always been an advocate of magnanimity in victory and on behalf of the Government and their supporters I wish formally to announce that we give Mr Morgan Phillips complete release from his obligations.'

Despite everything we were forging ahead with the preparation of a full statement of Party policy based on the decisions at Morecombe and on the reactions of local parties to our discussion notes. A two-day meeting of the full National Executive in December, under the excellent chairmanship of Arthur Greenwood, gave detailed and objective consideration to the problems likely to face a future Labour Government. Our next task was to obtain the full co-operation of the Trades Union Congress, but in this we were not entirely successful. At a meeting with Labour's National Executive on the 9th January 1953 the TUC proved unwilling to have a joint statement on nationalisation and economic affairs ready by April. These discussions were mainly cordial, but a few speakers on both sides obscured the main issues with debating points.

In the following weeks these debating points grew in number. The magazine *Tribune* castigated Lincoln Evans of the Iron & Steel Trades Confederation for accepting a knighthood. In the *Daily Telegraph*, Sir Will Lawther the TUC President described Bevanite activities as 'a deliberate attempt to undermine the leadership in the same way as Hitler and the Communists did'.

Stern action was clearly needed. At a four-and-a-half-hour meeting in February, the National Executive decided to complain to the TUC about Will Lawther; Arthur Greenwood described his statement as 'in many ways quite wrong and unnecessarily offensive'. The Executive also judged the *Tribune* Brains Trust as 'contrary to the spirit and intentions of recent decisions by the Parliamentary Party'. Unfortunately the fighting continued on all sides.

On the evening of Monday the 26th April 1953, after a two-hour session of the National Executive, I was able to announce that the survey of the nation's problems and our proposals to meet them were ready for publication. Only one section of domestic policy remained unresolved: whether to nationalise the big chemical companies. The TUC had its doubts about such a move, so we decided to propose a government inquiry to see which parts of the industry would be best brought under public control. Jim Griffiths and I launched the policy document, now titled 'Challenge to Britain' on the 16th June.

Early in July, Herbert Morrison announced that he intended to stand against Arthur Greenwood for the post of Labour Party Treasurer. Will Lawther, still smarting at Greenwood's criticism of his *Daily Telegraph* interview, threw all his union's weight behind Morrison, whose reason for standing was to regain his place on the National Executive. The leaders of the Transport & General Workers and other anti-Bevanite union chiefs would have preferred Morrison as Treasurer rather than Arthur Greenwood, who refused to join either faction.

I was anxious to avoid a clash between two men who had done so much for Labour, and I hit upon a scheme. I asked Hugh Chevins of the *Daily Telegraph* to write that an amendment was being moved to allow the Deputy Leader (Morrison) to participate in National Executive meetings. At the same time I persuaded my friend Herbert Tracey to get his union colleagues to propose just such an amendment. Hugh's story and Herbert Tracey's counsels did the trick. The National Union of Seamen put the amendment on the Executive agenda, and it was carried. Herbert Morrison, satisfied, withdrew his candidature for Treasurer.

Almost the whole of the 1953 Annual Conference was spent on consideration of 'Challenge to Britain'. It has always been the Executive's right to decide who makes the official speech in each debate. In 1953 I was given the task of speaking on two of the most controversial issues, foreign affairs and reshaping our industry, and I took full advantage of this rare opportunity. It proved to be the last occasion on which I was allowed to address the Party Conference on anything other than organisation. No reason was ever given for this; I had some ideas of my own about it.

'Challenge to Britain' and the National Executive's statement on foreign affairs were both carried almost unanimously. Compared with 1952 it had been a good conference, and it had prepared the Party for the next general election. Now we had to present 'Challenge to Britain' to the voters. We arranged for Executive members to visit local parties, urging educational and organisational activities to publicise our policies. I addressed weekend meetings in many different localities, outlining the major features. 'Challenge to Britain' was available to the public from December.

Early in 1954 dissension arose once more over German re-armament. The foreign policy statement approved by the 1953 Conference put it like this:

> 'Conference urges that there should be no German re-armament before further efforts have been made to secure the peaceful re-unification of Germany.'

At the Berlin Conference (January-February 1954) the Foreign Ministers of Britain, France, the USA and the Soviet Union failed to reach agreement, mainly because the Russians refused to allow free elections in East Germany. The matter was due to be debated in the British House of Commons, and the Parliamentary Labour Party met on the 23rd February to decide what line to take. Our leader Clement Attlee believed that, as further efforts had been made to secure German re-unification, the Party would be within the spirit of the 1953 statement if it supported a measure of German re-armament. The Parliamentary Party approved of Attlee's plan by 113 votes to 104. Next day the National Executive passed a similar resolution by 16 votes to 9.

On the 15th April Nye Bevan resigned from the Shadow Cabinet, partly in protest at Attlee's cautious attitude to the Government's policy for South East Asia, but mainly to lead the campaign against German re-armament. The strife became more and more bitter, and the arguments more and more personal.

Arthur Greenwood died on the 9th June. To my mind he was the most underrated figure in the whole history of the British Labour Party. His altruism and his sound common sense brought inestimable benefits and he was sorely missed.

With his death the post of Treasurer fell vacant. As the appointment could only be made by the Annual Conference, I acted as Treasurer until September. There were two candidates, Hugh Gaitskell and Nye Bevan, who gave up his Executive place to stand. When the election was held, Gaitskell received 4,338,000 to Nye's 2,032,000. Having resigned from the Shadow Cabinet and the National Executive, Nye was now completely excluded from the higher counsels of the Party. Although some of his troubles were of his own making it is not surprising that he felt bitter when he spoke at a *Tribune* meeting the day after his defeat:

'I know that the right kind of leader is a desiccated calculating machine who must not allow himself in any way to be swayed by emotion.'

The bickering continued and the party's morale slumped. My staff and I worked under considerable difficulties and were constantly accused by the Right and the Left of showing a bias. It was an achievement just to keep the Party alive. Nye Bevan himself avoided further controversy until the 9th February 1955, when he urged the Parliamentary Labour Party to call for four-power talks before the final ratification of the Paris agreements on German re-armament. His idea was rejected by 93 votes to 70, whereupon he organised an unofficial motion. His action compelled the PLP to pass a strongly worded motion against him. Finally in the Defence Debate on the 2nd March he challenged Attlee on the floor of the House to state that the Hydrogen Bomb would not be used to meet an attack by conventional weapons, a challenge that Attlee rightly ignored. Two weeks later the Party whip was withdrawn from Nye Bevan and the National Executive, at its meeting on the 23rd March, made his conduct a subject for discussion.

Several right-wingers, especially Arthur Deakin, wanted him expelled from the Labour Party. Nye came to see me in my office just before the meeting and asked me frankly, as an old friend, what his chances were. I told him, 'It'll be a close thing but I think you'll be all right.' It certainly was close; by 14 votes to 13 the Executive decided that Nye should just be requested to prepare a statement on his conduct, for consideration by a special sub-committee. Attlee had voted in Nye's favour.

Shortly afterwards the national newspapers were closed down by a strike, and the whole affair was allowed to blow over, which was just as well because we were soon involved in a general election.

✳ ✳ ✳

1955 and the Penny Farthing

On the 5th April 1955 Winston Churchill resigned as Prime Minister. Nine days later his successor Anthony Eden announced that a General Election would be held on Thursday the 26th May. Dick Crossman, Tom Driberg and I were asked to write the Party manifesto, which we published on the 29th April, just a fortnight after Eden's announcement. Over 2,000,000 copies were issued and the manifesto was acknowledged as 'briefer and much more readable than its Conservative counterpart' (David Butler: British General Election of 1955).

The campaign was slow warming up. Squabbles inside the Party had robbed many people of their enthusiasm and it proved difficult to stir up excitement. Each week of the campaign the Gallup Poll showed the Tories moving further ahead. We simply did not have the will to win.

Polling day passed uneventfully. When the results started coming in, it became clear that the Tories would be returned with an increased majority. We lost 18 seats and our percentage of the total poll fell to 46.3. As usual, I prepared a campaign report for the first National Executive meeting after the Election on the 22nd June. In it I warned against isolating one factor as being responsible for election results, but I admitted that after four years of comparative prosperity many industrial workers, 'whilst they would not in any circumstances vote Tory were happy about the present position and had no inclination to secure a change of government this time'. There were no real issues sufficient to stir the conscience of the electorate. The Party's internal disputes probably did not much affect the voters but they did serious harm to the morale of our volunteer workers. In consequence, the canvassing and the organisation both suffered. As I put it: 'Any decline in the keenness of individuals to do voluntary work for the Party in and out of election times is bound to affect the voting strength of the Movement.'

This was a very important point. Our permanent organisation had been in no way inferior to that of 1945, 1950 or 1951 but there had been far less enthusiasm among voluntary workers.

Hugh Gaitskell had told me before the June meeting that several members of the National Executive wanted an intensive investigation into the Party's organisation across the country, and he asked if I had any objection. I felt that by no means all the Executive realised the difficulties under which the paid staff had to work, and I offered to give every assistance. So I was not surprised when the Executive, after considering my report, selected Harold Wilson, Jack Cooper, Arthur Skeffington and Margaret Herbison to form a fact-finding committee on organisation and produce an interim report by September. I did regret that so much time was being spent on discussing organisation to the exclusion of the rest of my report.

A few days after the meeting, the sub-committee invited me to have lunch with them at St Ermin's Hotel. It was a pleasant occasion but I was asked very little, so I assumed that they would contact me later. In fact I never heard from them again, with the result that neither I nor anyone else at Labour Party Headquarters was allowed to supply any relevant information. We were not shown the interim report until five days before it was due to be considered by the National Executive, and only then because Harold Wilson's committee wanted us to duplicate it for them. On Monday the 26th September, two days before the meeting and while we were delivering copies to Executive members, the *Daily Mirror* printed a full and accurate summary of the committee's finding, obviously from a copy of the document, and gave it the heading LABOUR PARTY BOMBSHELL.

I can only guess why the report was leaked to the Mirror, but the *Irish Times* surmised:

'This leak has gravely embarrassed the Labour leaders; for so strong is the report that they have withheld formal endorsement of it and called for certain revisions. In other circumstances the report might have been hushed up and never published.'

The National Executive was now forced not only to publish it, which was an unusual step in itself, but also to put it on the agenda for discussion at the Annual Conference.

When the report was officially published, the newspapers joyfully hailed what they not unnaturally regarded as an attack on Transport House. With headlines like 'Penny-Farthing Machine' and 'Socialists Under The Microscope' they swooped on the most damning features. They all quoted the final paragraph:

> 'After what we have seen of Party organisation throughout the country our surprise is not that the General Election was lost but that we won so many seats as we did. We were particularly disturbed by what appears to be the progressive deterioration of the Party's organisation, especially at constituency level...'

An organisation based on volunteers can always be said to be penny-farthing in a jet age. First, you have not got full-time workers. Second, you have not got a modern office that is properly equipped. It is perhaps a typewriter in the secretary's home. But when you're an officer of a party and they say you're responsible for the machine to blame, it's a very difficult thing to say they are wrong, because it will seem as if you are objecting to new ideas.

The public accusations of inefficiency at Transport House and in the constituencies not only depressed party members; they also caused voters to wonder if a political party that managed its own affairs so badly could be trusted to govern the country. True, three of the 143 paragraphs of the report referred to other factors in our defeat but (in heavy black type) 'the fact remains that compared with our opponents we are still at the penny-farthing stage in a jet propelled era, and our machine, at that, is getting rusty and deteriorating with age'.

The *Daily Telegraph*'s interpretation is worth recording:

> 'At this coming Conservative Conference it might well be asked how, with the Socialist organisation in such a parlous state, only 15 seats were gained during the Election.'

The report was discussed during the private session of the 1955 Annual Conference. Harold Wilson spoke first, then came a full debate in which many delegates took part. Wilson and his colleagues cannot have been entirely satisfied with how the debate went. Few speakers discussed the committee's recommendations and several delegates, particularly from urban constituencies, criticised the methods by which the report had been compiled. There were complaints about its inaccuracies. Nye Bevan attributed the General Election defeat to the lack of a true socialist policy. The overall view was that the finest organisation was doomed to fail without the backing of a united and enthusiastic party.

After the debate I took a press conference and was surprised to learn that the private session had been relayed by loudspeakers to the sun lounge of the Winter Gardens, to which everyone had access. This meant that journalists were even better informed than usual about the 'private' session. One reporter asked whether Nye's speech had lasted longer than the regulation five minutes. I told him it had lasted for a Welsh five minutes, a remark that received as much publicity as anything that happened that afternoon.

Subsequently, the London Labour Party asked those members who had stood as candidates in the Election to give their views. Of the six who responded, five cited Tory prosperity as the main factor in Labour's defeat. Four mentioned the quarrels within the Party and four the lack of awareness of socialist principles. There was only one complaint about organisation and that related to the postal vote. Three praised the organisation, with one saying, 'Some of the complaints about bad organisation must be discounted as coming from local parties which failed to mobilise their own resources properly.'

Of course I had long been aware that the party needed to spend more money in this direction. The salaries paid to our officials were, without exception, disgracefully low, and in our propaganda and other activities we were constantly hindered by a shortage of funds. The National Executive did agree to act on some of the committee's recommendations. Early in 1956, plans were announced for 13 organising assistants to be appointed to support the party's regional organisers and for 30 agents to be employed in marginal constituencies. Canvassers would be paid and voluntary workers given training. However, the proposal to have a standing committee of the National Executive to supervise organisation, a committee from which the Labour Party Secretary was specifically excluded, was never implemented. Head Office did not need any sub-committee to supervise it. On the contrary, it would benefit from much greater freedom in managing the Party's affairs.

In the local elections of May 1956, before any changes had taken effect we gained 330 seats. This should have convinced the party that by far the most important factor in any election is the prevailing mood of the voters. We would be fooling ourselves if we believed that we could win just by spending more money. Indeed, the next General Election was going to dispel that fallacy.

A month after the 1955 general election, four Labour veterans – Hugh Dalton, Chuter Ede, Emanuel Shinwell and William Whiteley – all gave up their positions of responsibility in the Parliamentary Party. I am certain that they expected the party's leader Clem Attlee to resign with them, but he delayed his announcement for six months. He never confided to me or to any other colleague the timing of his resignation. There was no one whom he particularly wanted to succeed him and he knew that it was too late for Herbert Morrison to become leader. On the 8th December he asked me at short notice to arrange a press conference at Transport House. He made a two-minute statement briefly summarising his career and wishing his successor well. When someone asked whom he preferred to succeed him he struggled for quite a while to light his pipe, so eventually I told reporters that the result would be known very soon.

In the ballot Hugh Gaitskell, with 157 votes, had an absolute majority over his two opponents, Nye Bevan, with 70, and Herbert Morrison, with 40. Morrison promptly resigned as deputy leader. This meant that the posts of treasurer and deputy leader were now vacant. As the former appointment could only be made at the Annual Conference I reminded the National Executive of a constitutional precedent when Arthur Henderson had held three offices simultaneously – leader, secretary and treasurer. The Executive then decided that Gaitskell should hold the dual role of leader and treasurer until the Annual Conference. In the ballot for deputy leader Nye Bevan lost out again; Jim Griffiths won by 141 votes to 111. Two days later at a Tribune rally in Manchester, Nye made his opinion clear:

> 'If the Labour Party is not going to be a socialist party I do not want to lead it... When you join a team in the expectation you are going to play rugger you cannot expect to be enthusiastic if you are asked to play tiddly-winks.'

He poured scorn on the Wilson Report, saying that he for one did not want to go faster if the car was going over a precipice.

* * *

Law not War

In the summer of 1956, after Colonel Nasser had nationalised the Suez Canal, war between Egypt and Israel seemed inevitable. Labour's new leader Hugh Gaitskell made a reasoned and statesmanlike speech in the House of Commons on the 2nd August, warning the Government not to breach international law. However, when he declared that he did not object to the precautions taken by the Prime Minister up to that point, his words were widely misunderstood and misrepresented, so I restated the Party's attitude ten days later:

> 'It is up to us to convince the Egyptians that they have everything to gain by

co-operation with the many nations that use the canal. I do not believe that threats of duress – as distinct from ordinary precautions – can help us to achieve this aim... If the Egyptian government should refuse to adopt a reasonable course of co-operation with us all, our actions must then be governed by the fact that we are a member of the United Nations, that we are a signatory of the United Nations Charter and that we must not place ourselves in a position where we might be denounced by the United Nations as aggressors. Any action Britain might take as the circumstances became extreme should fully respect the spirit of the Charter.'

On the same day Gaitskell and I met Guy Mollet, the French Premier, at the French Embassy in London. He had come for consultations with the British Prime Minister, and he told us of his determination to keep in alignment with the UK Government over the Suez crisis. Mollet gave no indication of what their joint policy might be, but we remained unconvinced that the Tories, with their outdated philosophy, held the solution to the problem.

Gaitskell later discussed this with Erich Ollenhauer, leader of Germany's Social Democrats, Swedish Prime Minister Tage Erlander and Adolf Schaerf, Vice Chancellor of Austria. All three distinguished politicians wanted the British Labour Party to make clear its opposition to the use of force. This brought home to us our responsibilities not only to the British people, and the peoples of Israel and Egypt, but to democratic socialists all over the world, who were waiting to see us put our principles into practice.

On the 29th October, Israeli forces thrust deep into Egypt's Sinai Peninsula. On the 30th the notorious Anglo-French ultimatum was issued, demanding the withdrawal of Egyptian and Israeli forces from the Canal area and the occupation of key Canal points by British and French troops, an ultimatum that Nasser could never accept. The next day, British planes bombed Egyptian airfields.

In its gunboat diplomacy, the Conservative Government most emphatically did not have the support of the Labour Movement. At 10 am on the 1st November I reported to a special meeting of the National Executive that the Albert Hall had already accepted our provisional booking for a protest meeting to be held there in five days' time. The newly formed Suez Emergency Committee had also contacted me to see if the party would take over the organisation of a protest rally to be held in Trafalgar Square on Sunday the 4th November. The Executive agreed that my office could organise the rally. The Trades Union Congress and the Co-operative Union offered their full support for our 'Law Not War' campaign that was to be waged all over the country.

We were asked to supply speakers for 137 gatherings in one week, but the Trafalgar Square rally overshadowed them all. Some 15,000 people gathered there, many holding our 'Law Not War' banners, to hear speeches by Tony Greenwood, Frank Beswick, Edith Summerskill, Harry Nicholas and Nye Bevan. There was a collection, and the public's generous contributions enabled us to fund the campaign which helped bring the war to a close.

The only unfortunate consequence of our firm stand was the breach that it caused with our French comrades. As Chairman of the Socialist International I permitted a resolution charging the British and French Governments with breaking the UN Charter. The French delegation, led by Pierre Commin, walked out of the meeting. Pierre told me afterwards that I should not have allowed the resolution to go to a vote, as there was no prospect of the French supporting it. However, the general feeling was so strong that a vote could not have been avoided.

The National Executive had welcomed the Hungarian Revolution of 1956 and had sent a resolution to the Nagy Government hailing the restoration of democratic institutions, and the rebirth of the Social Democratic Party. That was before the Soviet Army began its ruthless attack on Budapest on the morning of Sunday the 4th November. The National Council of Labour (the co-ordinating body of the Labour Party, the TUC and the Co-op) wanted the Soviet Ambassador to receive a deputation making clear the views of the Labour Movement. I contacted the Ambassador, Mr Malik, and he agreed to meet us in two days' time. I prepared a two-page document reminding the Soviets of their acceptance the previous year of the ten principles laid down by the Afro-Asian Conference in Bandung, Indonesia. The intervention in Hungary had transgressed every one of these principles. Our document concluded:

> 'This delegation calls upon the Soviet Government instantly to abandon its policy of aggression and bloodshed in Hungary and to allow the Hungarian people the elementary right to decide their own future. It urges the Soviet Government to abide by the Bandung principles and United Nations Charter and thus to demonstrate before world opinion that the new policies proudly proclaimed during and since the 20th Party Congress have not been totally submerged'.

In reply Malik read out a long, prepared speech stating that the Russian troops had gone into Hungary at the invitation of the 'legal' Kadar Government to avert a fascist coup and restore order. He made no attempt to answer the points that we had raised, and Gaitskell told him that his answer was totally unacceptable. We realised we were wasting our time, and that our only hope was that he might pass the document to his master. In the meantime we launched a 'Help Hungary' fund, which drew a response of £11,417 from local parties, women's sections and youth sections alone.

* * *

Planning for 1959

At Labour's 1955 Annual Conference the National Executive promised that ten policy documents would be issued in the next three years. With a few modifications this plan was carried out. Four documents appeared in 1956 and five the following year. Finally, in 1958 we published 'Learning to Live', 'Plan for Progress', 'Prosper the Plough', 'Let Scotland Prosper' and 'Labour's Foreign Policy'. Looking back I realise that our programme was overambitious. Furthermore, by issuing so many policies, which went into so much detail, we aroused opposition on all sides and confused many of our own supporters. 'Industry and Society' (1957) in particular provoked fresh conflict between those party members who wanted more nationalisation and those who wanted less. Worse still it scared the iron and steel barons into financing a prolonged campaign against nationalisation. It would have been better if we had simply re-affirmed our belief in the common ownership of the basic industries.

After the Trades Union Congress moved from Transport House to brand new premises we gained more space. I was given a three-room suite on the ground floor for myself and my staff, and we also installed a £3000 television studio to enable us to present our case more effectively.

By July 1958 our programme of policy-making was complete, and I felt that we should begin immediate preparations for a general election. The National Executive authorised the necessary expenses. In November we produced a short policy statement 'The Future Labour Offers You' in a particularly attractive format and at a heavily subsidised price (6d). It was acclaimed by the party, and made a big hit with the general public. At the same time we arranged conferences to share ideas about publicising Labour policy and campaigning for support. I have no doubt that in this pre-election period the party's workers, voluntary and paid, made phenomenal efforts to win the electors over, in the face of our opponents' lavish anti-nationalisation campaign.

Early in 1959, as the election grew closer, I began to consider my own position. I was 56 years old, and I wanted a role that would involve less detailed work and more opportunities for creative service. Furthermore, I still nourished my lifelong ambition of becoming a Member of Parliament like my old schoolmaster from Bargoed, Morgan Jones. The Member for North East Derbyshire, a safe Labour seat, was not standing for re-election, and two local parties within the constituency had asked me if I would like them to nominate me as a prospective candidate. This was traditionally a miners' seat, and the Derbyshire Miners Council had already put forward its own nominee, a local councillor named Stanley Mellors.

The first two Labour Secretaries, Ramsay Macdonald and Arthur Henderson, had been MPs (and held high office in the Government), but since their time the party's rules had forbidden the Secretary from standing for Parliament. In any case it would have been difficult for me to campaign in the North while running the Election from London. On the 15th March I discussed the position with the Labour leader Hugh Gaitskell and his deputy Jim Griffiths. They were surprised that I was considering leaving Transport House but they raised no objections to my offering myself as a candidate. As an ex-miner, I was reluctant to stand against the official Derbyshire Miners' choice, but my plans received a setback in May when the doctors at West London Hospital told me that I might need surgery for a gall bladder complaint. I had to stay in hospital till mid-August, but fortunately I responded to treatment and did not have an operation.

My time in hospital coincided with a jury summons. I had originally been notified to prepare for service at the Old Bailey in April. If the Election had been called while I was on a jury, it could have left the party in a difficult position. I asked to be exempted on the grounds that I had publicly spoken against capital punishment, against treating homosexuality as a crime and (because of the Laski case) against the jury system. I did not gain exemption, but my summons was postponed.

My first public appearance after my illness was at Blackpool on the 6th September, just before the Trades Union Congress. All my union and newspaper friends commented on my weight loss (the effects of a low fat diet) and my refusal to drink anything stronger than lemonade. Actually I was feeling much fitter for my stay in hospital, and looking forward to the election.

A few days after Blackpool, I heard that Stanley Mellors had withdrawn his candidature in North East Derbyshire through ill heath before nominations closed. Unexpectedly, I was back in the running, together with Tom Swain, Ted Castle (Barbara's husband) and Malcolm Wynn, a teacher from Gleadless near Sheffield. The Derbyshire Miners made it clear that they supported Tom Swain. I talked the matter over with my wife Norah and with George Wright, a friend and colleague of mine for many years. Norah urged me to stay in the contest. If I was tied to London during the election, she would canvass for me in Derbyshire. George, however, wanted me to withdraw rather than incur the ignominy of being rejected by a constituency party. I considered my chances of election. If Ted Castle and Malcolm Wynn were eliminated in the first ballots I would need to pick up their votes if I hoped to defeat Tom Swain. Ted was a friend of mine, but his supporters were left-wingers and unlikely to vote for anyone connected with Transport House. It was only a chance, but I decided to go ahead with my nomination.

All four nominees spoke at the selection meeting in Chesterfield Market Hall, after which the delegates were asked to write down the name of their choice. These papers were collected for counting, and after a lengthy delay it was announced that Tom Swain had more votes than I, but not an absolute majority. Malcolm Wynn was eliminated and a second ballot held. Again it was indecisive. Ted Castle dropped out, so the third ballot was a straight fight between Tom Swain and me. I lost by 81 votes to 103.

I now realised that I had no chance of entering Parliament this time and that I would probably be too old when a future General Election came round. A lot of people wondered why I bothered to enter a contest that was a foregone conclusion from the start. I had withdrawn once in May, on health grounds. To withdraw again would have been a discourtesy to the Barlow and the Handley Labour Parties that had originally nominated me. I was aware that rejection might be bad publicity, but in the event the press coverage was sympathetic.

* * *

What are we going to say, Comrades?

On the 8th September 1959 the Conservative Government gave notice of a General Election on the 8th October. Hugh Gaitskell, the Labour leader, was in Moscow with Nye Bevan; they cut short their visit and returned the following day. The Labour National Executive met to approve the manifesto and plan the campaign. A special committee was established, consisting of Dick Crossman, Tom Driberg, Alice Bacon, Ray Gunter and me. Our job was to remain in London supplying daily propaganda material to our candidates and to the newspapers, radio and television.

The Conservatives had spent far in excess of anything we could afford to state their case on hoardings all over the country. To counter this we intended to exploit to the full the free publicity provided by the press and by broadcast news. Every day at 7 am I would release a statement for the early editions of the evening papers. At 10.30 am our campaign committee would decide on the line of attack for the day and at 11 am I would hold a press conference and issue fresh statements.

Even before our campaign had officially started we received some welcome publicity. Our hard-hitting pamphlet 'The Tory Swindle' was due for publication on the 11th September, but I received a three-page telegram from Randolph Churchill (Winston's son) claiming infringement of copyright, because his criticism of the Suez debacle was quoted without permission. Accordingly he was seeking an injunction.

A judge considered his request that same day and refused to grant the injunction. I was photographed outside the court proudly displaying 'The Tory Swindle'.

On Monday the 21st September I held the first of my daily press conferences. By the end of the week, according to Butler & Rose's 'British General Election of 1959', I had secured about 200 inches of space in the columns of the nine national dailies, more than ten times the amount given to the Conservatives. This was in many ways a turning point in the election. Lord Hailsham, Lord Poole and other high-ranking Tories took over the press conferences at Conservative Central Office, and sometimes held two sessions a day. On the evening of the 28th September, Hugh Gaitskell publicly pledged not to increase income tax 'so long as normal peacetime conditions continue'. The campaign committee had not advised him to say this. It was his personal rejoinder to 'How are you going to pay for it?' the invariable Tory cry whenever a reform was suggested. The newspapers hailed this as a major tactical blunder by Gaitskell, but I am sure it was the repeated question, not the pledge, that cost us votes.

In the campaign's second week we still got more press coverage than our rivals. On Thursday the 1st October my research department prepared a statement on purchase tax. Copies were issued to coincide with my press conference that morning, but because of a misunderstanding no one had informed me, so I made no mention of it. A number of reporters failed to get a copy, and a routine handout merely restating what Harold Wilson had often said in the Commons acquired an air of mystery and received far more publicity than it deserved. One newspaper even praised my acumen in deliberately ignoring the handout.

This was a television election with candidates from every region appearing on the screen. At the beginning of the campaign we secretly felt that people would not bother coming to meetings; they would be content to stay home and make up their minds there. Events proved us wrong. Gaitskell and others had bigger meetings than the Party had enjoyed in 1945.

With a week to go, I was happy about the way things were going despite my natural caution. As I said at the 1ˢᵗ October press conference, 'I have never felt more relaxed in any General Election campaign. This is the 1945 spirit manifesting itself ... One last spurt and we're home.' The *Daily Express* commented,

> 'The miners of North East Derbyshire did Mr Morgan Phillips a favour when they insisted three weeks ago in picking their own man as their Labour candidate. If they had said Yes to Mr Phillips he would have been just another candidate among the 1500.'

The Labour Party's morale was higher than at any time since our great 1945 victory. Unfortunately, we were trying in three weeks to overcome the effects on the electorate of a sustained campaign to convince them that life was better under the Conservatives. The nearer we came to polling day, the more people thought about prosperity, and the more they believed that Labour would in some way endanger it.

Field Marshall Lord Montgomery enlivened the final week by stating that anyone voting Labour 'must be completely barmy, absolutely off his rocker and should be locked in a lunatic asylum as a danger to the country.'

After I pointed out that 'if Labour voters had been locked up in lunatic asylums our potential Field Marshall would have been left without an army' he gracefully apologised.

On Election Day I stayed in my ground floor office by the phone in case any legal difficulty should crop up. I had two television sets, one for BBC, one for ITV. Two members of staff were recording the results as they came in. They had charts showing the safe seats and the marginals. The press were on the first floor, the radio room on the second. Many of my staff were working in their own constituencies, but after polling closed at 9 pm they returned to Transport House. Some were confident, others despondent. Privately, I was now not hopeful. Recent electoral setbacks in Belgium, West Germany and Australia were not good omens.

The first result came in at 10 pm. At Billericay in Essex the local party had acquitted itself well in the local elections but the General Election result proved disappointing. In a constituency that we needed to win we only managed to reduce the Conservative majority. Periodically I would go to the radio room, giving interviews to maintain the morale of supporters across the country, whilst knowing all the time that we had no chance now of winning. As more seats were declared it became clear that the Tories would retain power with more members than before.

Hugh Gaitskell rang me before midnight saying, 'Things aren't going too well, are they?'

'No,' I replied, 'I think we've had it.'

Not long after that, his PA John Harries rang for an update. I replied that he should inform Gaitskell and Nye Bevan that we would lose by 70 seats at least. Gaitskell responded by conceding victory to the Conservatives. Labour had lost its third consecutive election. There was a gap between the Party worker and the voter, and the gap was widening.

It was particularly disappointing that after thousands of pounds had been spent streamlining the so-called penny-farthing we had crashed far more disastrously than in 1955. Searle Wisden in the *Daily Mail* later published my off the cuff response: 'There's a new rider on the seat of the penny-farthing but, damn, it squeaks louder than ever.'

I shared the general disappointment but found consolation in the fact that some other person would have to be the scapegoat this time. My press conferences had won the Party an unrivalled amount of free publicity and had raised the status of the Party Secretary at a time when some were trying to reduce the importance of the office. The first meeting of the National Executive recorded its appreciation of the work of my staff and gave me a personal vote of thanks.

Within a few hours of the declaration of the result, the press rushed to deliver a funeral oration over the body of the Labour Party. Then, party members began presenting their own recipes for the future. The press, not to be outdone, quickly brought the corpse back to life: 'Labour Split Widens'. Political commentators breathed a sigh of relief; their jobs were safe for the foreseeable future.

As it turned out, most of the inquests centred on policy rather than organisation, and some wild ideas emerged. We were advised to drop nationalisation, drop socialism, change the party's name, break our ties with the unions, make a deal with the Liberals and recognise that capitalism had solved most of society's conspicuous evils. This prompted me to indulge in the luxury of a personal pronouncement when speaking to the Oxford University Labour Club on the 11ᵗʰ November 1959:

> 'The primary industries, whose level of efficiency and production and control of raw materials and services determine the economic pattern of our society and the level of activity of our secondary industries, ought to be publicly owned and operated in the national interest... The private sector should be required to respond to the public interest by such general controls as may be desirable. These will include physical and financial controls and planning powers.'

The Annual Conference had been cancelled because of the election. The National Executive decided to hold a weekend conference on the 28ᵗʰ and 29ᵗʰ October to discuss Labour's future. Apart from speeches by Hugh Gaitskell, Nye Bevan and Barbara Castle (the retiring Chairman of the National Executive), all the speakers would come from the floor.

In retrospect this conference should never have been held. All the speakers gave their own views, not the views of those whom they were representing. Furthermore, because they were not debating any precise resolution, the discussion wandered all over the place. There seemed to be little connection between the speeches of Hugh Gaitskell and Barbara Castle, or between those of Gaitskell and Nye Bevan.

Hugh's speech contained the unfortunate reference to Clause IV of Labour's Constitution, which defines one of the party objectives as securing 'for the workers by hand and by brain the full fruits of their industry and the most equitable distribution thereof that may be possible, upon the basis of the common ownership of the means of production, distribution and exchange, and the best obtainable system of popular administration and control of each industry or service'. Of this the leader said,

> 'Standing as it does on its own this cannot possibly be regarded as adequate. It lays us open to continual misrepresentation. It implies that common ownership is an end whereas in fact it is a means. It implies that the only precise object we have is nationalisation, whereas in fact we have many other socialist objectives.'

This was perfectly true, but it was the wrong time to say it. Some right-wingers in the party had already suggested dropping the idea of nationalisation altogether, and the ever-suspicious left-wingers took Gaitskell's remarks as a major step in that direction. The conference atmosphere grew progressively worse. The party, badly hurt, was tearing open its own wounds. Then Nye Bevan rose to make the final speech of the conference. He was to do what no one else could have done; he changed the prevailing mood from disillusionment and despair to hope and determination. At the 1947 Conference he had made a courageous speech, in 1958 a statesman-like one, but in 1959 he gave the finest and most important speech of his career:

> 'What are we going to say, comrades? Are we going to accept the defeat? Are we going to say to India, where socialism has been adopted as the official policy despite all the difficulties facing the Indian community, that the British Labour Movement has dropped socialism here? What are we going to say to the rest of the world? Are we going to send a message from this great Labour Movement, which is the mother and father of modern democracy and modern socialism, that we in Blackpool in 1959 have turned our backs on our principles because of a temporary unpopularity in a temporarily affluent society?'

Who heard these words and was unmoved? None of the cheering delegates can have dreamt that this was to be Nye's last public address. A truly great socialist and a truly great man, he died on the 6th July 1960.

✳ ✳ ✳

Labour in the 1960s

After Labour's 1959 Annual Conference I was asked by the National Executive to prepare a memorandum on the history of the party's Constitution, the fundamental principles involved and any alterations that suggested themselves. This was an agreeable task, as I had long favoured clarifying and streamlining the Constitution. Accordingly I presented three documents to the Executive on the 29th January 1960. The first described the development of the party from 1900 to the present, as illustrated by alterations and additions to the constitution over the years; it also gave a detailed history of the party's attitude to common ownership. The second document highlighted the sections that appeared to need redrafting, and the third contained my suggestions.

The National Executive decided to hold a special meeting on the 16th March to discuss the documents. In the meantime I conferred with the party's leader Hugh Gaitskell, and we agreed on a formula by which the restatement of Labour Party objectives could be attached to the existing Clause IV. At its March meeting the Executive adopted the restatement with certain amendments, and circulated it to affiliated organisations. Subsequently the Executive commended the restatement to the 1960 Annual Conference as a 'valuable expression of the aims of the Labour Party in the second half of the Century'. The Committee did not want to present Conference with any proposed amendments to the Constitution.

I hoped that consideration of the Constitution would be delayed for two years to allow a complete redrafting after full consultation with party members, and I prepared a discussion pamphlet for this purpose, but it was never issued. Instead I was asked to submit to the Executive a statement on the relationship between the Annual Conference, the National Executive and the Parliamentary Labour Party. This was published in August 1960.

I was also asked to make a report on my Head Office staff. I used this opportunity to request that my own position be made clear in view of recurrent rumours that I would have to share my responsibilities with someone else. In March 1960 the sub-committee reviewing my report recommended that the Secretary should play a greater role in forming and publicising party policy, and should enjoy closer liaison with the Parliamentary Labour Party. He should also have an administrative assistant for the more routine office work.

Inevitably the newspapers exaggerated this decision, calling me 'Overlord' and 'Monty Morgan' (ironic in view of my election clash with the original Monty). For me it was sufficient that my position had finally been clarified. I could now tackle the huge problems facing the party in my own way.

One of the first priorities was to build up the new Young Socialist movement. In speeches all over the country I urged local parties to allow and indeed encourage teenagers to play an active part in politics. It was unreasonable to expect young people always to toe the party line and never enjoy any apolitical activities, and it was criminal to give them all the donkeywork and no responsibility. I hoped that by 1964 at least one third of Annual Conference delegates would be under 26, and on the 11th April I announced to the press that the Labour National Executive would write this into the Constitution if the Young Socialist movement made good progress. At the same April press conference, I urged women to take their rightful place in politics:

> 'Women have greater social attributes than men but they lack the vanity of men, and after all you need some vanity in public life to stand the burdens.'

In June the Executive approved my preliminary plans for a Festival of Labour to be held in London in June 1962, which would embrace art, sculpture, music and drama, and have a particular appeal to progressive young men and women.

I had long felt it wrong that party members were entirely dependent on newspapers for information about Transport House and the National Executive. To remedy this situation I visualised a General Secretary's Newsletter, issued monthly, which would keep supporters informed of our plans and activities and supply the background to official statements and circulars. The first Newsletter appeared in May 1960. In all humility I was astonished by the response. Letters of appreciation and requests for extra copies flowed in from all over the country. Many said that the newsletter removed the sense of remoteness from Transport Hose and from the National Executive Committee, the activities of which they hardly knew until it made its annual report to Conference.

That May there were local elections, where we were defending over one thousand seats won in 1957. Only a miracle could bring further gains, and I warned the Executive that miracles were unlikely while party members were 'as angry as they are at present over the controversies raging in our ranks'. To have any hope of success we had to 'demand from both the National Executive Committee and the Parliamentary Labour Party a demonstration of unity and the active participation of all in the local elections'.

The controversies continued and we paid the price. My report to the Executive (25th May) was blunt:

> 'It would be easy for us to dismiss our setback in the current elections on the ground that we had not recovered from the 1959 General Election, but this overlooks the important fact that we ended our General Election campaign in good heart... Since November 1959 however there has been a sharp outbreak of controversy within the Party, at times conducted with unusual ferocity and acrimony that is having a devastating effect on the morale of our active workers. This has been reflected in a number of letters received at Head Office.
>
> We cannot afford to ignore this if we are to have any hope of winning the next General Election. I have always been convinced that the spirit of the Party in 1952 that occasioned so much depression at our Morecombe Conference in that year had disastrous effects on our prospects in 1955. If we are to prevent this sort of thing happening again we really must concentrate now on improving the morale of the Party.'

Because of my report I was asked to produce a paper on the state of the party for consideration by a special meeting. I presented this paper on the 13th July, and after detailed discussion the National Executive suggested that it could be redrafted and issued to the general public. When I had done the redrafting the Executive decided to endorse its action points and commend the whole document to the 1960 Annual

Conference. For the first time since 1953 I was to address Conference on a matter of vital importance to the Party.

In the document, published in August 1960 with the title 'Labour in the Sixties', I tried to turn the party's thoughts from the fruitless squabbles of the present to consideration of the problems that lay ahead of us: problems of policy, of membership and of the relationship with the unions:

> 'Only when the British people see a clear difference dividing Tories from Labour will they lose their reluctance... The central issue of politics throughout the world today is not merely how the new riches shall be distributed within and between the nations but, just as important, how the new powers released by science shall be controlled... When our opponents claim that socialism is outdated and must be scrapped, they are flying in the face of the facts. On the contrary, our socialist beliefs will be vindicated in the 1960s as it is ever more clearly seen that the new post-war capitalism is creating its own innumerable problems and that, in the epoch of the scientific revolution, democracy, if it is to survive, must plan its resources for the common good.'

The trade union scene had also been changed by the scientific revolution. There had been an expansion of employment in non-manual work, and non-manual workers would often shrink from joining a union. If they did form a group it would not necessarily affiliate to the Trades Union Congress, still less to the Labour Party. 'As a result our membership was gradually ceasing to be what in the past we have always claimed as its greatest strength – a mirror of the nation at work.' It was our immediate task to increase our membership among the 'expanding, industrial, occupational and social groups which will, in a measurable period of years, include the greater part of the nation.'

In the section on party membership I called for more political discussion at local level, brighter party premises, more pay for officials and a drive to recruit more women and young people. The party would need more money to carry out these essential improvements. I planned to ask the trade union leaders about stepping up affiliation fees.

I held a press conference on the 9th August to launch 'Labour in the Sixties', and it was a particularly enjoyable occasion for me. As one reporter put it,

> 'The General Secretary of the labour Party ... having been rolled in the dust and written off as dead by all sorts of people in the Labour Movement has now reached the summit of his comeback. 'Labour in the Sixties' is his new testament.' (*The Guardian*, 10th August 1960)

I had no doubts about my role. My friend Trevor Evans of the *Daily*

Express told me, 'It looks as if you will have to pull the party out of its crisis – even if you never become the leader.'

Trevor says that I 'accepted the first bit without immodesty and the second without demur'. Then he told me, 'you are a happy man because you know what you can do, yet you have stopped grieving for the unobtainable, and for a politician that is a miracle.'

'That's my secret,' I replied.

On the 15th August I flew to Scotland to record 'For Information Only', a television programme in which three journalists asked me questions about 'Labour in the Sixties'. As the programme progressed I felt that I was doing well. I had no warning of what was to come. Jean Macaulay, one of the three journalists, wrote in the *Daily Record* & *Mail*:

> 'The facts are that Morgan Phillips was in excellent form, was stimulated and stimulating, laughed, talked, smoked and enjoyed thoroughly the experience of answering questions because he believes so sincerely the views he puts forward'.

Later, after watching a playback of the recording I started out for my hotel in a car driven by a Scottish Television executive. Suddenly I began to choke. The choking grew worse and worse, and the car returned at high speed to the studios, where a doctor was called. By that time my right arm and leg were numb and my tongue was paralysed. The doctor summoned an ambulance, which rushed me to Glasgow's Western Infirmary. The only thing that I remember clearly is trying to get someone to phone my home.

* * *

Stroke

Of the eleven days that followed my collapse in Glasgow I have practically no recollection – only patches here and there, not amounting to anything. I do not remember my wife Norah and my children Gwyneth and Morgan visiting me every day in hospital. I do not remember hearing them read to me the hundreds of letters, cards and telegrams wishing me well. Nor do I recall the times when I was angry, upset or depressed, when I laughed or when I tried to speak or to read the newspapers. Yet, I am told, all these things happened and my family thought that I was aware of everything going on around me.

The TV programme was broadcast as planned on the night after my stroke. Thousands of Scottish viewers heard me say, '(Journalists) have been writing so long that I was dead and wouldn't lie down. Now they have discovered that I am alive' at a time when I was lying critically ill in hospital.

On the 26th August, eleven days after my stroke, the surgeons decided on an operation to remove a blood clot from my brain. This could only be performed at Killearn Hospital, 18 miles from Glasgow. I was moved by ambulance in the afternoon, and the operation took place early in the evening. Next morning saw a great improvement in my condition. My right arm and leg were still paralysed but I was entirely conscious of my surroundings. Though still unable to speak properly I could articulate one or two words. I was able to read and to listen to the radio, and I began to try writing with my left hand. Norah visited me daily and eventually she was allowed to take me outside in a wheel chair.

My biggest disappointment was that I would not be fit to introduce 'Labour in the Sixties' to the Party's Annual Conference. This increased my anxiety to get back to London, but despite my impatience I had to wait until Sunday the 9th October to be released from hospital. Back at home I made slow but steady progress, which sounds comforting but could not make up for the frustration caused by the limitations of

Festival Fanfare

movement and speech. There were encouraging landmarks like my first public appearance, to watch Fulham FC play Wolverhampton Wanderers on the 26th November, and a visit to my office before Christmas 1960. And I had many occasions to feel grateful for the help and guidance of my family and friends, who spent time with me, took me out for a drive and sent me books to read. I was able to contribute to the planning of the 1962 Festival of Labour, which I had announced before my stroke.

Unfortunately, my recovery, though pleasing my doctors and therapists, was too slow to satisfy me, and in December 1961 I informed Labour's National Executive that I was ready to give up the post of General Secretary. I made clear that I wanted to work for the party when my recovery was complete. In February 1962, eighteen years after becoming Secretary, I retired, having witnessed the rise of democratic socialism not only in Great Britain, but in countries as far apart as Bolivia and Burma.

Looking back over those eighteen years I could see more clearly than ever that the Labour party had been overwhelmed by its own committees. So many of them, so little to show for the time spent. Sometimes a committee failed to act on its own recommendations, sometimes it contradicted the findings of another committee. The only possible outcome was confusion.

Another cause of the party's malaise, the antagonism between right wing and left wing, constantly manifested in the committees of which I speak. Some people refused even to sit on the same committee, let alone reach agreement. All they achieved was to prevent anyone else making a decision. Certainly they re-united when an election was near, but at other times they were more interested in fighting each other.

It is an obvious if unpalatable truth that more tolerance was needed. The Bevanite faction originated from Clem Attlee's refusal to let Nye Bevan be himself, and so a ginger group became the unofficial opposition to the party's leaders. No one could claim that the left-wingers fulfil this latter function with any success. Rather they reflect the party as a whole, completely lacking inspiration and endlessly resolving themselves into cliques.

Anywhere in the world where there is injustice, hunger and the like there is a task for the Labour Party. The worldwide evil of race hatred and organised discrimination presents a savage challenge that only a strong and active socialist movement can meet and defeat. Our work has not ended. It has only just started. We might yet build a socialist society in Britain such as the movement's pioneers only dreamt of.

Editor's postscript

Morgan Phillips dictated his autobiography at various points in the 1950s. This resulted in a number of drafts. After his stroke in 1960 I helped him edit and complete the narrative, and prepare it for publication. My father died in January 1963 and the book never appeared in print. Recently my son Alexander came across a carbon copy of the complete text, which, having been checked against other drafts and against news cuttings, is at last made available to the public more than fifty years after it was written.

I have here added some notes of my own. Apart from Harold Laski's letter, these were not in the original manuscript. They are included here because they give information that may be helpful both to the casual reader and to anyone researching this important period of Labour history. In this section of the book, Morgan Phillips will be referred to as MP, as a reminder that this section is not autobiographical. This also means that my mother becomes Norah Phillips and my sister Gwyneth Phillips (later Dunwoody).

Morgan D Phillips

A family holiday 1952

Harold Laski's letter

See the chapter headed 'The Harold Laski Affair'. This is part of the letter that Harold Laski wrote on the 15th June 1945 for the attention of the National Executive Committee of the Labour Party. He was concerned that if Clement Attlee, the Labour leader and prospective Prime Minister, attended the Three Power Talks involving the victorious allies – the USA, the United Kingdom and the Soviet Union – he might be bound by undertakings given by the war-time Prime Minister Winston Churchill.

'I heard of Mr Churchill's invitation to Mr Attlee to join in the Three Power Talks at 6 o'clock in the BBC News of Thursday the 14th June. Mr Churchill gave no indication of the basis upon which he extended the invitation. It was unprecedented for a Prime Minister to invite the Leader of the Opposition to act in this way… I was disturbed by Mr Churchill's remarks on 'continuity of foreign policy' and upon the identity of outlook between himself and Mr Attlee on all international matters while they were in the same Cabinet… I felt that the relation of Mr Attlee to such a meeting might well be argued to imply a commitment, express or tacit, to any agreements reached at the meeting. Many of the decisions would be secret; the ultimate communiqué would reveal little beyond general and vague formulae; therefore the Party, which might well be a Government after the 27th July, might find itself bound, especially in the eye of the USSR and the USA by 'understandings' of which Mr Attlee alone was cognisant and about which he only had seen the relevant documents.

I tried to get in touch with Mr Attlee during the evening on four occasions, but vainly… I then felt it was of the first importance to make it clear that responsibility for any decisions at the July talks would be Mr Churchill's and not Mr Attlee's. Otherwise we should be leaving it open to be assumed, as Mr Churchill's speech had indicated, that they were in full accord on all matters of foreign policy …

It is no use supposing that the Tories would sympathise with a Left France, with an Italy or Spain which strove to free itself from the trammels of monarchy and dictatorship, or with the governments in any country which sought to take over key industries and resources for the use of the common people. But I do assume that these tendencies would be supported by the Labour Party and not less by a Labour Government. I believe further that they would be supported by the USSR if only out of its interest in its own security…

We seek to use our victory, both at home and abroad, for ends the Tories do not approve, by methods they reject. I do not think we gain by allowing the electorate, nor indeed public opinion abroad, to forget this. Socialism is not a minor variation on a Tory theme; it is a body of general principles as well as immediate policies that is different in kind. We ought to say so forthrightly.'

MP persuaded Laski to neither send this letter nor to make it public, because the Conservatives could use it in the election campaign to undermine Attlee's authority. As it was, Churchill wrote a six-page letter to Attlee on the 2nd July 1945 and made it public the next day, quoting from Laski's speeches and commenting:

'I certainly expected, as the days passed by with repeated effronteries, that you would make some effort to establish your position against Mr Laski, and that he would in some way be disavowed by his Committee or by the Labour Party as a whole. Nothing like this has however occurred and we are left in the position that he has given you instructions that you have personally rejected but which nevertheless remain the official, authoritative and re-iterated instructions of the Executive Committee of the Labour Party. This manifestation of where the real power rests raises far-reaching considerations.'

As MP makes clear, the whole anti-Laski campaign made little impact on the voters.

* * *

Harold Wilson's letter

In December 1961, MP decided that his recovery from the major stroke was taking too long for him to have hopes of resuming as Party Secretary. He notified the Party's National Executive, who discussed the situation and asked Party Chairman Harold Wilson to communicate their decision. Wilson visited him at his home and told him he need have no worry about money and that there would be an important role for him in the party when he was fit. Subsequently Norah Phillips, MP's wife, wrote to thank him for the reassurances. This is Harold Wilson's reply, dated 30th January 1962:

'Dear Norah,
Very many thanks for your letter. You really should not have troubled to write.

Referring to my successive visits to Rannoch Road may I express my warm thanks to you and Morgan for the very great understanding you both showed, despite the feelings that must have been going through Morgan's mind. I am glad that the NEC in the event were able to come to their decisions with so much unanimity and with such a spontaneous resolution of appreciation for all Morgan has so far done for the party.

The other thing that pleased both Dai [Davies] and myself was the progressive improvement in Morgan's condition as visit succeeded visit – especially, though Dai was not with me – last time.

You can be sure that all Morgan's colleagues will be desirous of using to the full the great reservoir of experience and judgment which Morgan still brings to the service of the party.

Yours, Harold'

* * *

Morgan Phillips's letter

Nine months later, on the 1st November 1962, MP dictated this letter to be sent to the new Chairman Dai Davies:

'Dear Dai,

As you know I have always tried to cooperate with the National Executive Committee but I have reached the stage when I feel that certain matters must be placed on record.

1) As you know it was decided to appoint my successor on the 7th March 1962. In actual fact this was done on the 28th February and from that day without any notice my salary ceased.

2) I understand from reading the newspapers that a resolution had been carried at the NEC meeting expressing appreciation of my services. I do not know whether this information is correct or not as so far I have not received any letter to this effect. In fact the only letter I have received was sent to me in late September as a result of my meeting [Fred] Mulley at a football match when he asked if I was going to Annual Conference and I said that I did not know as I had not been invited. He told me he would look into this matter and the official letter was the result.

3) Until the Festival of Labour in June I was in constant touch with the office two or three days each week through the organiser, Mr Merlyn Rees, and he used the car as and when he wished. I understand that before the Conference the NEC agreed that the office should take possession of the car. I had asked about this when the new General Secretary was appointed in February and was told to keep it for the time being. On the 19th October I received a curt intimation that it would be collected one day in the following week.

It appears that it is not considered necessary to give me notice of anything, I appreciate that some people may be glad to be rid of me but there is a decent way to do this. I am happy to say that while I was General Secretary matters of this kind were dealt with in a completely different way.'

The draft ends at this point and it is not known whether the letter was ever completed and sent.

Notes on specific chapters

A visit to Winston Churchill

'We were running a conference each evening for the exiled socialist parties of occupied Europe.' The story of how this conference led eventually to the rebirth of the Socialist International with MP as its first Chairman is told in *Socialist International* by *Morgan Phillips*, which follows *Labour Party Secretary* in this volume.

A Bargoed childhood

Remarkably there is a 1921 picture of the Bargoed Independent Labour Party in *A History of Bargoed and Gilfach: Vol. 2* by *Paul Jones* (Old Bakehouse Publications, 1998). MP stands at the back, bareheaded. His mother Sophie is on his left. I have no other pictures of MP before his engagement photo in 1929. I did not have any shots of his mother (nor of his brother Billy), so I was very grateful to receive some lovely photos from Mr D J Horton and Mrs Gwenllian Horton (nee John).

MP's sister Elsie, cousin Annie and mother (Sophie)

The Labour college

George Phippen, who was a fellow student of Nye Bevan (1919-21), gives a fine description of the Labour College in the 1974 edition of *Aneurin Bevan 1897-1945* by Michael Foot (Paladin).

Research department

'If the invasion had come anywhere between Grimsby and Southend'; this remark is strangely precise. Perhaps MP, writing in the 1950s, was conscious of the Official Secrets Act. L L Margetts in *The Post* (16th August 1952) has a more dramatic version:

> 'A German invasion was at that time considered imminent, and no-one realised more the vulnerability of the Fen Country, with its miles of open coastline, than did Morgan Phillips. He also realised, perhaps better than most, that if East Anglia was occupied some sort of underground resistance would have to be organised. He therefore drew up plans for a network of resistance groups throughout the area.'

Nye Bevan

As a long-time family friend, Nye Bevan attended the wedding of MP's daughter Gwyneth to Dr John Dunwoody in May 1954. However, three months later Bevan publicly humiliated MP while they were on a Labour Party delegation to China. MP later recounted this to Hugh Gaitskell, Bevan's rival for the Party leadership, and apparently added his opinion that the left-winger 'was now finished' (*The Diary of Hugh Gaitskell 1945-56*, Jonathan Cape, 1983).

Nye at Gwyneth's wedding

I do not know if any reconciliation took place but politically Bevan redeemed himself from his mid-1950s low point. His contempt for the Wilson Report must have delighted MP.

'Two men who had done so much for the Party.' All the references in this book to Herbert Morrison are positive. Kenneth O Morgan's first-rate chapter on MP in *Labour People* (Oxford University Press, 1987) writes of 'a close but sometimes uneasy relationship with Morrison (whom Phillips tended to feel had upstaged him in the 1945 campaign)'. He based this statement on interviews with my mother. One of the cartoonist Vicky's many brilliant concepts showed MP as a publican (which was indeed one of his plans for retirement) with two customers Herbert Morrison and Nye Bevan. The caption read. 'One mild, one bitter.' The publican was a mild man too.

'My staff and I worked under considerable difficulties'. Having risen through the ranks MP knew that his hard-working, dedicated office staff were underpaid and too often undervalued. He was a popular if mercurial boss, always ready to lend a sympathetic ear and give support where needed. One of his staff will have done the research for this book, almost certainly Rose Davy, who had served the Party for many, many

Office staff (Rose Davy on the extreme right)

years, had an encyclopaedic knowledge of its history and did vital work on Labour's archives.

1955 and the Penny Farthing

Norah Phillips was waiting outside the Conference Hall during the closed discussion. A trade unionist, one of the first to leave, winked at her and said, 'Vox populi.' Party members were not interested in looking for a scapegoat.

What are we going to say, Comrades?

As an office junior employed during the election, I manned an information room, giving out leaflets, posters and press releases to members of the public visiting Transport House. One morning an agency reporter came in to use the phone. When he spotted the press release on purchase tax he (very honestly) told me, 'That shouldn't be here. It hasn't been released yet.'

I phoned Arthur Bax, the Press Officer, who admitted that the document should have been distributed at that morning's press conference. A simple error had been made and it was amusing to see how some commentators devised conspiratorial theories about the incident, some praising my father, some scorning him. After MP's death it was revealed that Arthur Bax 'was working for several Soviet bloc intelligence services' (Christopher Andrew, *Defence of the Realm: The Authorised Story of MI5*, Allen Lane, 2009). Since MP had many friends in Special Branch he may have been aware of this.

This chapter shows MP's true feelings about Nye Bevan. Just before the election, MP was asked by a close friend whether Labour would win. He hesitated, then replied, 'We could with Nye as leader.' MP was deeply moved by Bevan's death in July 1960 and he worked day and night to ensure that the great socialist had a fitting send-off. With Bevan gone he surely felt that the onus had transferred to him to save the Labour Party – only for a severe stroke to silence him just a month later.

Part 2

Socialist International

By
Morgan Phillips

Introduction

On a bleak day in January 1915, a few months into the First World War, I sat down at a desk in a South Wales schoolroom and began to work earnestly at an exam paper. Success in that exam meant a lot to me for it would give me the right – at the age of 12 – to go to work and earn a few shillings.

The Labour Examination had been introduced so that boys with a reasonable standard of education could be released from school to help the war effort. It was a great day for me when I learnt that I had passed the exam and could work alongside my mates. In every family in those coal mining villages the urge to be out earning wages had long transcended all other considerations.

Work was plentiful but hard. We were tough youngsters and we savoured every minute of our newfound independence. Then came the Armistice, the bonfires and dancing in the streets, but in the shadows the spectre of unemployment was preparing to haunt our communities again.

I had been working in the pits since June 1916, my fourteenth birthday. It meant little to me when the price of coal began to sag but in March 1921 our world collapsed. Collieries closed and I was one of many to draw a last wage packet and trudge away from the pit. The vast army of the jobless was making a mockery of the peace that had been won so dearly.

By that time I was an active member of the labour movement. We organised the unemployed into an association demanding relief work, meals and shoes for children and an improvement in relief scales. Despite our best efforts hope started to fade as the unemployment figure for South Wales reached a quarter of a million.

The mine owners, quick to take advantage of our poverty, demanded a reversion from the national wage agreement to the old system of district agreements, which meant a heavy cut in wage standards. The miners refused and then began the infamous lock-out of 1921. Ironically I and many other unemployed people were fortunate for we continued to draw the dole, while our comrades who were locked out received no strike pay at all. Inevitably the men were defeated and there was still no work for us.

Our week would go something like this. On Monday, Wednesday and Friday we would queue to sign on at the Labour Exchange, then proceed to the Workmen's Institute to scan the wanted advertisements in the daily papers, hoping that someone somewhere would have a job for one of us.

We would spend the rest of these days walking up and down the main street or standing on the street corners with our older colleagues, many of whose households had begun to break up with the departure of the daughters to domestic service in London. The routine on Tuesday and Thursday was a little varied. We would trudge round the pits that were still open, hoping that our luck would perhaps turn.

The evenings were generally taken up with vigorous political work at the local branch of the Independent Labour Party, in evening classes or at the occasional dance. Our socialism was something vital and urgent; our sworn enemies were unemployment, victimisation, poverty and the anarchical system that made these possible.

So the wasted years dragged on until 1926, when the mine owners demanded a longer working day and lower wages, and the entire trade union movement of this country rose to defend their comrades. To the end of my life I shall remember the great Miners' Conference at the Kingsway Hall, London, on the 29th April 1926, when we waited for the decision of the unions' executives. Nor will I forget that most magnificent of all May Day demonstrations, which marched seemingly without end up Kingsway while we waited.

Then came the dramatic news that the workers of Britain were with us in our great struggle. At midnight on the 2nd May they would stop work throughout the country so that we might win with justice.

With tremendous feelings of elation and gratitude we returned to our homes, determined to fight for our wages and for our families. The slogan 'Not a minute on the day, not a penny off our pay' swept through the country. But we did not win. The General Strike ended without an acceptable settlement, leaving us to fight on alone for many bitter months until finally we had to give in.

I little dreamt then that this would be my last fight in that coalfield. A few months later I won a scholarship offered by my union, the South Wales Miners' Federation, which took me far from the scene of my early struggles.

I left my hometown Bargoed for London, and finally I found myself working to organise and strengthen the political power without which the Labour Party could never govern the country.

Morgan Phillips
General Secretary of the Labour Party 1944-1962
Chairman of the Socialist International 1952-1957

Europe after liberation

It has always been a pleasurable duty for the British Labour Party to make contacts with left-wing groups all over the world, sounding out their opinions and providing guidance where requested. During the wartime coalition and the post-war Labour Government the Party's ministers were not allowed to go abroad on party business. The party leader Clement Attlee was most emphatic on this point. Hugh Dalton proposed a motion at the Party's international sub-committee enforcing this rule, with the result that I, being Labour's General Secretary and not a member of the government, became the leading agent for foreign contact.

In October 1944 I had the fascinating experience of visiting Paris just after the Liberation to attend the Congress of the French Socialist Party. My companions were Harold Laski, George Dallas and William Gillies, all members of the international sub-committee. There was hardly any traffic in Paris, and George and I stood for twenty minutes in the middle of the road at the Place de la Concorde discussing domestic politics.

Many stories were told of the great heroism shown by the resistance movements in the countries occupied by the Nazis and their allies, and it was an honour to meet the French socialists as they emerged from the underground. Among them was Vincent Auriol, later to become French President. The conference elected him as party leader but in his acceptance speech he stressed repeatedly that he would only continue in the role until his fellow socialist Leon Blum could be freed from a German prison camp to take up his rightful place in French politics.

I have three strong memories from that conference: Auriol's love for France, the deep sincerity of his socialist convictions, and his great personal affection for Leon Blum. Fortunately the two men were reunited before Blum's death.

Blum, the party's leader since the assassination of Jean Jaures in 1914, was Prime Minister of France's Popular Front Government of 1936-37, which carried out notable and lasting reforms. In March 1942 the Vichy Government charged Blum with high treason, but by his courageous and eloquent defence he put his accusers in the dock and compelled an abrupt end to the trial. He was handed over to the Germans, and he spent the rest of the war in concentration camps.

After his release in 1945 he resumed the leadership and a year later he visited Britain for the Labour Annual Conference. His exquisite speech on the plight of socialists in Europe was beautifully translated for the delegates by Philip Noel-Baker.

Another great French socialist was the veteran Salomon Grumbach, who was born in 1884 and had represented Alsace in the German Reichstag before the First World War. His loyalty to France was complete but in two periods of German occupation he had avoided arrest. As Harold Laski put it, if the Nazis had condemned him to death he would have talked and talked until the firing squad died of old age. Salomon had a different explanation of his survival:

> 'I have a good stomach, a good appetite, a good morale and a good humour. But more than that, I was so young in the socialist movement – at 17 in Alsace when it was under the yoke of the Germans. It is my old socialist experience that has kept me tough and enabled me to survive all the tempests'.

He would also boast of standing up to Lenin at the time of the Kienthal 1916 Conference of Socialists against the war. When he died in July 1952 he was justly hailed by Kurt Schumacher the German socialist as one of the most powerful forces for understanding between the peoples of France and Germany.

In this context I must mention my close friend Louis Levy, who represented the French Socialists in London until his death in February 1952. Just as Salomon Grumbach worked untiringly for Franco-German understanding, so Louis sought to bring France and Britain closer together. He was so fond of this country that after his death his wife agreed to have him interred in Highgate. Subsequently his body was taken to France, where a second funeral was held. As I said on that sad occasion, Louis was 'a great socialist, a fine ambassador, a rich and lovable personality'.

The vast majority of European socialists underwent severe hardships during the Second World War, and when peace was declared all were faced by immense political and economic problems in their own countries, yet the prevailing mood was optimism. I was particularly aware of this when I visited the Danish and Norwegian socialists in August 1945 as a fraternal delegate to their conferences.

In Denmark the Prime Minister Vilhelm Buhl invited all the fraternal delegates to a reception. Inevitably, with so many socialists in one place, there was a tendency to talk shop. I was with Torsten Nilsson, the jovial Swedish Minister of Communications, and he shared my view that the proceedings were far too solemn. To liven things up we decided to start singing – fortunately Torsten knew as many songs as I did – and we launched into a medley including 'Ilkla Moor' and 'Drink To Me Only With Thine Eyes'. The other delegates were caught off balance but soon joined in with songs of their own countries. It turned into the most joyful gathering of international socialists that I ever experienced.

My closest friends in Denmark were H. C. Hansen (later Prime Minister in succession to another great socialist, Hans Hedtoft) and Alsing Andersen, a future Chairman of the Socialist International. These two, who had done so much for socialism in Denmark and in Europe, were inseparable until Hansen's untimely death in February 1960.

When I was in Oslo in August 1946 as a fraternal delegate to the Norwegian Labour Party Conference, I had the pleasure of meeting the Prime Minster Einar Gerhardsen. Einar, like me, began work at the age of 12 as an errand boy. Five years later he became a road worker, an occupation that he resumed in 1940 to cover his activities for the resistance. Another Norwegian socialist to resist the Nazi occupiers was Oscar Torp. In 1940 as Finance Minster he smuggled the nation's gold reserves out of the capital in 27 trucks and had them conveyed to Britain. He later succeeded Einar Gerhardsen as Prime Minister. It is sometimes forgotten that Trygve Lie, the first Secretary General of the United Nations (1946-53) was a leading Norwegian socialist. When I met him in 1945 he was Norway's Foreign Minister.

British socialists are justly proud of the achievements of their Labour Movement, so how much greater pride our Scandinavian counterparts must feel towards their heritage. In Norway and Denmark they have held office for extensive periods and have bestowed countless benefits upon their peoples. Even in Finland, with its unhappy history, there has been encouraging progress. In Sweden, which maintained neutrality during the Second World War, the socialists participated in government almost without interruption from 1932. Tage Erlander, who became Prime Minister of Sweden in 1946 at the age of 45, embodied all the enthusiasm, sagacity and high ideals of Scandinavian socialism.

The politicians in these four countries made Scandinavia the envy of Europe and a beacon to socialists all over the world

* * *

Towards a new Socialist International

In the eighteen years that I served as General Secretary of the British Labour Party (1944-62) I was fortunate enough to witness and to play a small part in the rebirth of the Socialist International, an organisation with the potential as yet unrealised of bringing peace, prosperity and unity to the world.

The first International had begun as far back as the 28th September 1864, when the London Trades Council and the Paris Workingmen's Committee held a mass meeting at St Martin's Hall, London, in support of the Polish Revolution. A number of political refugees from Europe attended, Karl Marx among them, and a French resolution to create an international association was carried and subsequently put into effect.

The new organisation was neither large nor wealthy, but in the twelve years of its existence it spread throughout Europe ideas of social justice, which brought terror to the ruling classes, and hope to the oppressed. Socialism was a growing force, and delegates from twenty countries assembled in Paris on the 14th July 1889, the centenary of the storming of the Bastille, to re-institute the Socialist International. Liebknecht, Edward Anseele, Keir Hardie, William Morris and Klara Zetkin were some of the legendary figures present.

Although this Second International was initially concerned with improving the conditions of the working class, it became increasingly preoccupied with the threat of war and the dangers of the arms race. When war did come in 1914, the International could not survive intact. Some members felt bound to help the war effort of their respective countries, while others strongly opposed the conflict. Not even the arrival of peace could repair the fragmented International, for in 1919 the Communists created their own organisation, and some socialists disliked the idea of acting in opposition to them.

Finally in 1923 a new Labour and Socialist International appeared, representing 43 democratic socialist parties. This new organisation attempted to become a closely-knit union, capable of really effective action, and to make majority decisions binding upon all members. In the troubled years that followed the LSI was able to help many victims of persecution, notably in Austria, Italy and Spain, until the Second World War made its existence impossible. The last meeting of its executive committee was held in Brussels in March 1940, a few weeks before the Germans entered the city.

During the Second World War a number of left-wing refugees were living in Britain. Johan Albarda for example had been President of the Dutch Parliamentary Party for fifteen years, and in 1939 he had succeeded Louis de Brouckère as President of the Labour and Socialist International. He spent the war years in London, serving the Dutch Government-in-exile as Minister of Public Works, Air and Transport.

The British Labour Party set up two special liaison committees to hold regular meetings, and on the 8th September 1944 received a request from the Inter-Allied Consultative Committee to take the initiative in preparing for post-war international socialist relations.

At its meeting on the 13th September our National Executive Committee agreed to convene a series of meetings in conjunction with the Party's Annual Conference. Each evening, after the close of the daily session, a number of British and foreign spokesmen adjourned to a nearby hotel to hold the first international conference of socialists from liberated Europe.

1944 was my first year as General Secretary of the British Labour Party, and the international gathering was a memorable occasion for all of us involved. Only a few months before, nearly the whole of Europe had lain under the heels of the Nazis, but now the forces of freedom were marching to final victory. Though still in the shadow of war we were meeting to prepare the foundations of a renewed international socialism. Delegates attended from France, Belgium, Italy, Sweden and Switzerland together with representatives (then resident in London) from Czechoslovakia, Poland, Norway, Palestine and Spain.

A further gathering at Transport House, London, over the weekend of the 3rd-5th March 1945 discussed a wide range of topics including international security, relief and rehabilitation. The following resolution was approved:

'The Socialist Groups represented at this conference are resolved to give new life to the Socialist International'.

A committee was set up to produce detailed proposals. It was agreed that Camille Huysmans should chair the committee and that the two other ex-Presidents of the Labour and Socialist International (Louis de Brouckère and Johan Willem Albarda) should be individual members, together with a delegate from each of Great Britain, France, Norway, Holland, Belgium, Poland, Sweden, Czechoslovakia, Luxemburg, Palestine, Italy and Spain.

When the war ended in 1945, Britain was not the only country to elect a socialist government. In Norway and Sweden the Social Democrats were in power, and Denmark, Austria, Belgium and France all had coalition governments in which socialists were represented. The success of our sister parties encouraged us to take the initiative in working towards a new Socialist International.

The Labour and Socialist International that had existed before the war had many defects: it prohibited the attendance of ministers, it tried to make its decisions binding on all countries, it excluded association with communist parties and it carried on a bitter struggle against the Comintern. That was in the past. The USSR had been our ally in the war against Fascism and the Comintern had been disbanded. Many on the left feared that any attempt to recreate the old LSI would be regarded as anti-Soviet, particularly if it tried to make decisions binding on all parties regardless of their state of development.

Clearly one of the first essentials was to establish good relations with the USSR. Recognition of this had prompted the National Executive of the British Labour Party at its Annual Conference in 1942 to decide on sending a representative goodwill delegation to the Soviet Union at the earliest opportunity. Harold Laski among others believed that it might be possible to build a single international organisation integrating the socialist forces of Europe, including the Russian working class. He told the Conference with the authority of the National Executive:

> 'The future of the whole of civilisation depends upon the establishment of a permanent basis of friendship with the Soviet Union. (The National Executive) should ask the authorities in the Soviet Union to receive a delegation from the British Labour Party for the purpose of discussing all outstanding problems between them and ourselves, and of finding, if we can find, a common basis that will enable their purposes and our purposes to march jointly together in an unbreakable union and for all time'.

Before the war the Communists, believing that they had the only solution to the world's problems, saw it as their duty to destroy the social democratic movement. Would it be their attitude now that there was unity in war to defeat fascism? Laski and I discussed this question many times, not only among ourselves but with the European socialists that had escaped to Britain during the war. Among them were three former Presidents of the old Labour and Socialist International, Camille Huysmans and Louis de Brouckère (Belgium) and Johan Albarda (Holland).

Many socialists were profoundly sceptical about the possible results of an approach to Stalin, but thought on the whole that an effort should be made, preferably by the British Labour Party. However the Coalition Government was unhappy about allowing any such official delegation. Anthony Eden told me privately that he favoured any attempt to get close to the Russian bear but Churchill was strongly opposed. The visit of the delegation was deferred until 1946.

In May of that year the British Labour Party convened an international conference at Clacton, which was attended by delegates from the Argentine Republic, Austria, Belgium, Canada, Czechoslovakia,

Denmark, Finland, France, Italy, Holland, Hungary, New Zealand, Norway, Palestine, Poland, Romania, Sweden and Switzerland. The parties from the four Eastern European countries were all working in coalition with the communists. The delegates took turns to speak about the political situation in their countries. For Britain, Hugh Dalton reasserted that the Labour Party had always recognised the need for close relations between the Soviet Union, Great Britain, the USA and France. A treaty of friendship with the Soviet Union had to be made a reality. Nevertheless, the Labour Party had resisted the constant attempts of the Communist Party to affiliate with Labour, and had always opposed the 'United Front' tactic.

In the discussion that followed, delegates from Eastern Europe pointed out that as the Red Army had liberated their countries the Communist Party had become a strong political force. In Czechoslovakia for example the Communists had 900,000 party members compared with 400,000 Social Democrats. The Eastern European delegates felt it essential to co-operate with the Communist Parties to build a socialist democracy and to prevent the re-emergence of revolutionary fascist governments. Similar views had been expressed in France because of the communists' role in the anti-Nazi resistance, but long before the Clacton conference the French Socialist Party had realised the impossibility of such a policy.

Salomon Grumbach, the French delegate, made a strong plea for the reconstruction of the Socialist International. The British and the Scandinavian parties, whilst anxious for the closest contact between socialists of different countries, were reluctant to recreate the same kind of formalistic organisation that had existed before the war.

After extensive discussion the conference agreed that a full-time socialist information office should be established in London. The British Labour Party accepted responsibility for administering the office, selecting the personnel and taking on the initial financial responsibility. Later when the extent of the financial commitment was known, the cost would be met by contributions from all the parties concerned.

It was agreed to convene again in the autumn of 1946. The German Socialist Party, the SPD, would not be invited, but delegates were urged to investigate the political situation in post-war Germany.

This further conference took place in Bournemouth (8th-10th November 1946), presided over by Emanuel Shinwell, then Chairman of the British Labour Party's National Executive. It established a consultative committee to prepare all future conferences and to advise on the production of an international bulletin.

With the formal business completed, the conference considered the problem of Germany. As I had recently visited the country, Shinwell called upon me to open the discussion. I appealed to those parties that were Germany's neighbours to help the SPD with office equipment and other materials needed to enable the party to function. My British colleagues and I had already approached our government about restoring property to the SDP that had been seized by the Nazis.

I recognised that some delegates were fearful of suffering political disadvantage in their own countries if they advocated the admission of the Germans to any future conference. I pointed out that our conference was a loose organisation for consultation without formal rules and without voting rights. Taking into account the difficulties facing the SPD and the duty of all members of the conference to safeguard the future of German socialism, I appealed to the delegates to welcome the SPD back into our midst.

As the discussion proceeded, it was clear that the representatives from Eastern Europe would be embarrassed if the issue were decided then and there. We agreed to discuss the matter further at the next conference, which would be held in Zurich. The leaders of the SPD would be invited to state their views and to answer questions. The Polish delegate voted against this proposal, and those representing Hungary, Czechoslovakia, Palestine and Romania abstained. Although I had proposed the SPD's readmission, I was anxious not to alienate the parties from Eastern Europe and Palestine. We urgently wanted them to stay in our ranks.

At the Clacton and Bournemouth Conferences it was generally understood that all decisions on policy should be unanimous while decisions on procedure needed only a simple majority. The opposition of the Poles alone was sufficient at Bournemouth to prevent a discussion on the German problem. So long as this rule obtained, one country would be able to block the admission of any party applying for membership.

When the Zurich conference met (6th-9th June 1947) the following resolution was proposed:

> 'The admission of new member parties shall be decided by a majority of two thirds of parties voting, provided that not more than half of the parties present abstain'.

This was passed by thirteen votes to four. The parties from Eastern Europe realised that the German SPD was likely to be admitted, but probably felt that so long as their opposition was on record their standing would not suffer in their own countries. We sincerely welcomed this change in their attitude.

Kurt Schumacher, the SPD leader, came away from Zurich with the public support of nine major European parties. There was a particularly strong plea for the SPD's admission from Salomon Grumbach, the French delegate.

At the same conference the Belgian delegate argued strongly for a new Socialist International. After detailed consideration the conference agreed that the time had come 'to envisage the reconstruction of the Socialist International'.

The Antwerp Conference (28th November-1st December 1947) was the last attended by delegates from the East. We saw clearly that a single International would be impossible at that time. When the conference tried to form a common socialist policy on peace and economic reconstruction, the Dutch abstained because the proposed statement made too many concessions to the parties from Eastern Europe, and the Poles, the Hungarians and the Italians abstained for the opposite reason. Only Czechoslovakia from the East supported the statement.

On the admission of the German SPD to future conferences, twelve parties voted in favour and four against – a decisive majority. The Germans were in at last.

The same conference set up an administrative committee (Comisco) with one representative from each party. I was elected to chair Comisco. When this new committee sat in March 1948 the communists had already seized power in Czechoslovakia and Romania, and none of the Eastern European parties sent representatives. Comisco voted to bar the parties of Romania, Bulgaria, Hungary and Czechoslovakia because their leaders had let them be absorbed by the communists. It appealed to the Italians and the Poles not to betray themselves in the same way.

In November 1948 Casimir Puzak, secretary-general of the Polish Socialist Party since 1921, and five of his comrades were put on trial for being anti-Soviet and for provoking opposition to the regime. In Bulgaria Kosta Lulchev, leader of the Social Democrats, and seven of his executive received gaol sentences ranging from ten years to life for trying to reorganise the Peasant Party and giving misleading accounts of conditions in their country.

Their fate was a terrible lesson to all who still believed that communism and socialism had something in common. The truth had never been more clear.

Morgan Phillips

Russia the Dark Crystal

On Sunday 28th July 1946 I was part of the Labour Party delegation embarking on a long awaited visit to the Soviet Union. With me were Harold Laski, Harold Clay and Alice Bacon.

The visit was a thrilling prospect for us all, but for Harold Laski it was something more. He deeply regretted the pre-war conflict between the Comintern and the Labour and Socialist International, and he believed that the time was right to build a single organisation, in which the Russians could play a full part. He had often discussed this with me, and he was undeterred by the fact that I and many other socialists were deeply sceptical of the idea. For my part, as Secretary of the Labour Party I wanted to see at first hand the results of a socialist administration that had been in power for nearly 30 years.

After leaving London we changed planes in Berlin and flew the rest of the way in a Red Army Dakota. Our fellow passengers were Russian soldiers and their wives returning from Germany. Four armchairs had been installed for our comfort, but the Russians had not thought to secure them in any way, with the result that we slid around during the flight.

The steward was a friendly fellow, who showed a liking for my English cigarettes. After each smoke he threw the burning cigarette end out of the window, just above the wing. Alice Bacon took a poor view of this, and I must admit I shared her fears for the safety of the plane.

As we flew over the areas of devastation between Berlin and Moscow, my mind was filled with conflicting thoughts. When I was a teenager in South Wales, the communists had contested an election there. I remembered arguing the merits of democracy against the dictatorship of the proletariat. Generally the Russian Revolution was regarded by British workers as one of the most beneficent acts in modern history. The British Labour Movement did not hesitate to oppose the Lloyd George Government's ill-advised efforts to interfere by organised intervention. Indeed the Labour Party's threat of direct action in 1920 was decisive in bringing to an end that reactionary political adventure. Throughout the interwar years the British Labour Party sought the fullest understanding with the Soviet Union. The attempted Anglo-Russian Treaty of 1924 was perhaps the major event in foreign relations of the first British Labour Government, and the re-establishment of relations with Russia was almost the first act of the second Labour Government in 1929.

After Hitler's advent to power, our party was insistent that friendship with the Soviet Union was a vital condition of peace, and we opposed the policies of successive governments that tried to evade that conclusion. The Labour Party was symbolised by Arthur Henderson, who for ten years – from the 1924 Geneva Protocol to the end of the Disarmament Conference – nobly strove in vain to find the terms of an enduring peace.

British socialists were stunned when the Soviet Union, having previously opposed the designs of Hitler, signed the Russo-German pact in 1939, and did not merely denounce the Allied Nations as imperialist but actually organised the parties of the Comintern to work against the war effort in democratic countries. Stalin seriously underestimated the ability of democracies like the United Kingdom to fight for independence in the face of what seemed overwhelming strength. Hitler also deceived himself when he assumed that the Western World would accept him if he donned the mantle of the anti-Bolshevik crusader. Britain was not prepared to tolerate the Nazis. When Hitler turned against Russia, the 22nd June 1941 saw the forging of a new partnership between Great Britain and the Soviet Union, something for which British socialists had been striving since 1917.

The few outsiders allowed to visit the Soviet Union were either so hostile to communism that they thought everything evil, or wore rose-tinted spectacles and believed that the people had found their Elysium. Admittedly it was difficult to take an objective view and objectivity was essential if we were to assess the industrial progress and the quality of life in the Soviet Union by western standards. When H. G. Wells visited Russia in 1920 he described the country as 'this dark crystal'. Though the confusion and chaos of the revolution had disappeared, the phrase was still apt in 1946 because most of the events since H. G. Wells visited were clouded in obscurity.

On arrival in Moscow we were met by representatives of the Russian Foreign Office, the Moscow Soviet and the British Embassy, and we faced an army of newsreel and press photographers. Later that day Vladimir Dekanozov, the Third Minister of Foreign Affairs, gave us our official welcome. His superiors, Mr Molotov and Mr Vishinski, were in Paris at the time. We told Mr Dekanozov that neither Russia nor Britain could afford to be sidetracked from the work of socialist reconstruction by mutual fears and suspicions. Common understanding could be a decisive factor in preserving the peace of the world. To that end we wished to meet the political, industrial and intellectual leaders of Russia.

On the following day Mr Popov, Chairman of the Moscow Soviet, welcomed us to the City Chambers. On the delegation's behalf I thanked Mr Popov and his deputy for their hospitality and introduced my colleagues, explaining which section of the labour movement each one represented. I emphasised that we had not come on a sightseeing mission. Our visit arose from the desire of the British people for friendship with the peoples of the USSR. In Britain the newly elected Labour Government was charged with transforming a war economy into a socialist economy. The unprecedented destruction in wartime and the widespread shortage of materials and manpower could only be overcome by a huge, united effort. There might at times be differences of opinion between Britain and Russia, but with real understanding such differences could fall into their proper perspective.

Mr Popov echoed our desire for friendship but could not discuss the political questions that I had raised. When I tried to press him I realised that he could not respond without serious embarrassment to himself. Finally we settled for a description of the work of the Moscow Soviet and the city's problems.

The following morning we met Mr Shvernik, the President of the USSR, in his Kremlin suite. He evinced great interest in the British Labour Government's progress and raised a number of points. The President then described the domestic difficulties facing the USSR and the steps taken to overcome them. He outlined their structure of government, which in his view had been tested in the course of the War by a powerful and ruthless enemy, and had stood the test. Large areas of

Mr Shvernik, Harold Laski and Morgan listening to the discussion

the country had been devastated, creating a terrific problem of reconstruction, both in industry and in the provision of homes. Despite the state's efforts some people were still living in dugouts. A large part of the national resources would have to be devoted to rehabilitating and reconstructing the industrial towns.

Shvernik believed that the War had proved the wisdom of collective farming. Under any other system Russia would have been in danger of defeat through a shortage of food. Instead, production was carried on by women and young boys and girls, who were imbued with the will to win through.

The Government's new five-year plan aimed to restore the mechanisation of industry to its pre-war level. If the weather remained reasonable, that year's harvest should enable them to relieve the acute food shortage throughout the country.

We ended the session with an agreement that any interruption to the work of rebuilding due to international uncertainty would be inimical to the interests of the people. Jointly we could ensure that there was no such interruption.

From the Kremlin we proceeded to a lunch arranged by the Chairman of the Moscow Soviet. We were able to talk freely with various ministers and leaders in the political, industrial and educational fields. By this time however I was aware that every conversation ended with a desire for friendship, couched in very general terms. Our hosts' only detailed contributions concerned the huge practical problems affecting the internal economy of the Soviet Union. When we raised specific points about co-operation between our countries we were sidetracked.

I tackled Mr Dekanozov about the Soviet refusal to let the Russian wives of British servicemen join their husbands in Britain. At first he claimed not to understand why Britons should want to marry foreigners – why could they not choose women of their own nationality? When I commented that this was a strange question for an international socialist to make, he laughed heartily and added that foreigners usually did not marry the best representatives of Soviet life. It was impossible to take the conversation further.

It was then arranged that we should meet the Chairman of the All-Union Central Council. We were greeted by Mr Kuznitsov and his colleagues, male and female. We emphasised that we did not represent the British TUC, but we were keenly interested in the work and development of the Russian unions.

Our hosts asked us many questions about the British Labour

Movement and then explained the structure of their unions, how they worked and what problems they faced. In industry the basic or minimum wage was set by the Soviets. The trade unions were involved in incentive payments, safety and welfare, and the provision of cultural and recreational activities. They were particularly proud of their work in connection with hospitals, convalescent homes, holiday centres and other places of rest and recreation.

So far as welfare was concerned the Russian worker seemed to be well catered for, but the workers' organisations could not be regarded as trade unions in the British sense. The very fact that strikes were illegal disposed of any pretence of freedom of action as we know it.

Our inquiries about schools were promptly met with a proposal that we go to the Ministry of Education to find out for ourselves. Through shortage of time we were unable to study the system in action but we realised from a cursory survey that a tremendous amount of care, thought and money had been devoted to education from the earliest days of the Revolution, when illiteracy in Russia was 70%. Education was a magic word to the newly freed peasant and worker, and the adults' desire to learn reading and writing led to the use of railway waiting rooms as schools. In a single generation illiteracy had virtually been wiped out.

War's tragic aftermath had brought thousands of orphanages into being. These institutions, some originally the homes of Tsarist nobility, must have evoked memories for veterans of the revolution, for in the days of civil war, famine and plague that followed many orphaned children ran wild, often forming into robber bands to obtain food. They were eventually gathered in by the government and educated into being good citizens by soldier-teachers, as immortalised in Anton Makarenko's great and moving novel *The Road to Life.*

I do not pretend to be able to write comprehensively about Russia after a visit of only 13 days. Alongside the sumptuous Moscow underground railway and the streamlined cars that slide through the wide streets I saw the barefoot, poorly dressed peasants selling fruit and vegetables. In comparison with the luxury standards of our sojourn in the capital there were the meagre, overcrowded living conditions of the vast majority of the population, with two or even three families sharing one room. But let it be remembered that war devastation in Russia was as in no other country. Even the worst blitzed areas of the United Kingdom would be lost on the trackless desert of smashed towns and villages left by the invading Germans.

A foreigner walking through the big shopping centres would certainly

Harold Laski, Alice Bacon and Morgan outside the Mayakosky station in Moscow

have thought that the Russian people wanted for nothing in the way of consumer goods. Yet the luxuries and many necessities were only available to those with money to burn. These shops did have the effect of eliminating the black market and giving the state the benefit of those rare customers who were willing to buy at any price.

A highly complicated system of distribution prevented me from learning how much an item like soap, sugar or a pair of socks might cost. It depended on who you were and where you bought them. Every factory hand was guaranteed supplies at reasonable prices whereas the office worker had no such privilege. Discrepancies such as this were partly responsible for the continuation of the 'Russian enigma' legend.

* * *

Joseph Stalin

During our 1946 visit to Russia we were eager to meet the Chairman of the Council of Ministers of the USSR, Joseph Stalin. After our talk with Mr Dekanozov, the Third Minister of Foreign Affairs, we were confident that such a meeting would indeed take place. It entailed a third visit to the Kremlin, where we had previously gone for a sightseeing tour and for a discussion with President Shvernik. By this time our faces were familiar to the Captain of the Guard, who met us at the gates. We were taken into the building and up the stairs to a quietly furnished but extremely comfortable waiting room. At nine o'clock on the evening of the 7th August 1946 we were greeted by the leader of the Russian people, who came walking towards us with his hand outstretched.

Stalin was simply dressed, much smaller and somewhat older than I expected, but his merry smile welcomed us before he said a word. There was nothing formal about the meeting; we sat at a table with the interpreter at the end, Stalin, Harold Laski and Dekanozov on one side and Harold Clay, Alice Bacon and I on the other. It was a large panelled room, thickly carpeted and decorated in neutral shades. Among the few pictures on the walls was a striking portrait of Lenin addressing an open-air meeting. The table had been prepared with paper, pencils, cigarettes and matches. There were no refreshments, nor did we expect any.

We talked in an easy conversational manner for two hours and a quarter. We were probing, trying to find out his ideas about the post-war world, how he saw it developing and what part he intended to play in it. One of the first things that I noticed about Stalin was that he had one habit in common with our Prime Minister Clem Attlee. He was a doodler and throughout the conversation he drew patterns on his writing pad with a blue pencil.

Early in the discussion I told him that while we wanted mutual understanding, we did not collaborate with the Communists in Britain. He seemed surprised. When I was outlining the Labour Party's plans for nationalising the coal industry, Stalin interrupted me to ask if we were not afraid that the dispossessed coal-owners would organise a counter-revolution. This was too much for my friend Harold Laski, who embarked on a dissertation about the strength of British democracy. He supported his argument with quotations from Voltaire and Diderot. Stalin allowed him to finish, then retorted, "Ah yes, Professor Laski, but Voltaire and Diderot had no coalmine owners to deal with".

The idea of mine owners organising a counter-revolution was laughable. We wondered if he really understood the British character. Similarly he marvelled at the way we came to hold India with so few men. To him it was one of the inexplicable things in world politics, a huge continent of millions of people kept within an Empire with a very small force. But there was a constant recurrence of a twinkle in his eyes. He enjoyed our jokes and his own.

He made no secret of his intense dislike and distrust of Winston Churchill, who had already (in 1919) tried to instigate war against the Soviet Union, and in the Russians' opinion was still attempting to do this. When we assured him that no one could drag us into a war contrary to the desires of the people, he reminded us that twenty years previously he had been visited by George Bernard Shaw and Lady Astor. The latter voiced her belief that Churchill was most unlikely to regain his political power, to which Stalin replied that if Britain was in peril of invasion, Winston would be called upon to save the country. Events, Stalin claimed, had proved him correct. He still regarded Churchill as a formidable defender of the rights and privileges of the forces of reaction. Winston's intervention after the Communist Revolution had bedevilled the relationship of our two countries ever since.

At the close Stalin expressed his satisfaction that both countries were travelling in the socialist direction. The Russian way, he believed, was shorter but more difficult because of the destruction of old institutions and the effects of war and revolution and had involved bloodshed. The British way was more roundabout but he conceded that we had a habit of reaching our destination. The Russian road to socialism was not necessarily better but in Stalin's view it was much quicker. In Britain, through the Parliamentary system, he explained, it was possible to sound the opinion of every responsible person as to whether he wanted socialism or not. In Russia in the early days there was a very low level of culture and the peasants, who were a great problem, did not want to hear about socialism. It was essential that we understood these indigenous questions.

Experience in Russia had shown that by nationalising the basic industries, together with banking and commerce, and devoting part of the profits to reducing prices and improving living conditions, and part to the expansion of industry, the Soviet Government achieved the double benefit of lower prices for consumers and a rise in the quantity and variety of production. On the whole he did not think that in Britain we had anything like the difficulties that had faced Russia after the Revolution.

This is only a fragment of our two-and-a-quarter-hour discussion, but I regard it as important to record Stalin's view on the two roads to socialism. There seemed to be a measure of agreement between us. Of course our experience since the end of World War Two has not been very encouraging. If the Soviet Foreign Office had really recognised that each country has the right to build its own socialist economy, its response to Ernest Bevin's 'Left can speak better to Left' would have been very different, and we should not have had to devote so much of our national wealth to armaments. I reported the conversation to Ernest Bevin, who in those days believed that if Stalin could accept an American presence in Europe, then Britain and the Soviet Union could rebuild not only Europe but the Middle East and other parts of the world too. He stressed to me: "Don't be harsh in your writings, don't say anything that is likely to upset, keep it friendly". The Russians were highly sensitive and difficult to handle, and undue criticism would add to the problems that Bevin had to face when dealing with them.

From Moscow we moved on to Stalingrad, where we met some of the best representatives of Russian life. Our young and vigorous hosts showed us with immense pride the sword presented to the city by HM George VI as a tribute to the heroism of its inhabitants. It was a magnificent piece of work.

We toured Stalingrad and saw something of the havoc wrought there. Our companions (civic dignitaries and Red Army officers) relived for our benefit many of the battles in which they had participated. I was amazed how much progress had been made in reconstruction since the defeat of Germany. We visited factories, crèches and many more new buildings essential to the life of an organised community.

At night there was a lavish banquet presided over by the mayor of the city. Afterwards our hosts broke into song with beautiful renditions of traditional airs. Then, to my horror, they wanted us to reciprocate. My three fellow delegates had many gifts but were reluctant to sing in public, so I stood up and delivered *Sospan Fach*, which was greeted with applause and requests for more. The mayor embraced me and hailed me as a baritone – so polite but so untrue. Then I tried the campfire song *One finger, one thumb, keep moving.*

Physically I was perspiring. August in Stalingrad was stiflingly hot and it was an ordeal to stand up and sing in a smoky and crowded room. Realising my discomfort, Harold Laski with his kind heart started to sing one of the few songs in his repertoire. It was an old election song mocking the Conservative politician Joseph Chamberlain, and each verse ended:

'I hear their angry voices crying
No more Joe'.

Beneath a huge picture of Joseph Stalin he got through four verses before he saw our embarrassment and sat down promptly. The official interpreter leant over to me and said, "It's all right, Mr Phillips. I will not translate".

We proceeded to Leningrad where once again we experienced great hospitality. We did a good deal of sightseeing, visited the opera and had many talks and far too many substantial meals. The most eerie event was at the railway station when we were due to return to Moscow. There were thousands of people assembled outside and we had to pass through them. Not a word was uttered, not a cheer raised though we were accompanied by the leaders of the city and representatives of the Soviet Foreign Office. I am still puzzled by that silent demonstration. It was so different from all our other experiences in the Soviet Union.

For our final evening the Soviet Foreign Office arranged a large party in our honour, attended by leading citizens from Russian politics, industry, culture and entertainment and members of the British embassy staff. During the evening I was dancing with a famous film actress of the Soviet film industry while her husband, the chief film producer, chatted to a British journalist who was working in Moscow producing *British Ally*, an English language newspaper for Russian citizens. I had visited the paper's offices and been very impressed by the achievement of the small staff and by its enthusiastic reception all over the Soviet Union. I gathered that some issues fetched very high prices on the black market.

When the dance ended we walked back to our table to find the British journalist and the Russian producer engaged in a lively discussion. They turned to me and asked if I had really been a coal miner. I assured them that I had, and showed the blue scars that every coal miner bears. These caused consternation among the Russian guests, who had obviously assumed that the British Labour Party was led by reactionary bourgeois elements.

We returned to the National Hotel to find some large cardboard boxes adorned with red stars. These were for us to take home. They were sealed and I left mine unopened because I could not see how I could close it again. I did not break the seal until we got back to London. The large box contained a writing set complete with two table lamps, an ink well and an ashtray, all in Russian malachite, a marble substance of considerable weight. Luckily my family met me off the plane, as I could never have carried these gifts home by myself.

* * *

Warsaw and Berlin

From Moscow we travelled to Warsaw at the invitation of the long-established Polish Socialist Party. Its unity had been severely strained in the final year of the war by divisions between the Government in exile and the Lubin Government set up by the Soviet Union. Many Polish

Socialists refused to collaborate with the Communist Party, which was backed by the Red Army. However Jozef Cyrankiewicz, the acting leader of the Socialist Party, saw friendship with the Soviet Union and an alliance with the Communist Party as essential. He had argued this strongly when I first met him in Prague in October 1945. He believed that his party could retain its independence and emerge as the stronger of the two in the alliance. I had expressed serious doubts, and when I landed in Warsaw none of the Polish Socialists tried to justify the policy to me. The problems that I anticipated had already occurred. Communists held the key posts in the government, and the army officers were Moscow trained.

The Socialists, though under pressure from local communist groups for even closer integration, wanted to preserve Poland's independence and to have friendly relations with the West. Further, they wanted to participate in a reconstituted Socialist International and to share ideas with the British Labour Party. I doubted whether the Soviet Union would allow this, but we promised to do everything in our power.

Sadly my doubts proved to be well founded. In August 1946 the Socialist Party had to expel its own Minister of Information, who had turned out to be a crypto-communist. Subsequently Prime Minister Osóbka-Morawski himself was expelled from the Socialist Executive for

Prime Minister Edward Osobka-Moraski sitting between Alice Bacon and Morgan Phillips

similar disloyalty. Jozef Cyrankiewicz replaced him as PM.

In the Polish Government half the cabinet ministers were socialist, but as usual the Communist Party held the Ministries of the Interior and of Defence. The Communists, alarmed by the growing strength of their rivals, demanded a complete fusion of the two parties. When this was rejected, they put similar pressure on the Co-operative Movement and on the Socialist Youth Movement. Despite Cyrankiewicz's public reaffirmation that his party would not merge with the Communists whatever interests they shared, the Socialists went the way of all social democratic parties in Eastern Europe. The lion devoured the lamb.

The circumstances of our delegation's departure from Warsaw showed how hard it could be to understand the workings of the Russian mind. We had booked to fly on a British Transport Command plane to London via Berlin. Our luggage was sent across to the collecting centre at the British Embassy, and then we had a final coffee with Osóbka-Morawski and Cyrankiewicz. When we reached the airport, a representative of the Soviet Embassy informed us that our plane would arrive in ten minutes. I pointed to the British plane and told him that our luggage was already on board. He insisted that a special flight had been arranged for us, and sure enough a plane had flown all the way from Moscow to take us on the two-hour trip to Berlin.

It turned out that the replacement flight was more comfortable, because the Russians could fly above the clouds while the British were restricted to a lower, more turbulent height. Even so, I was nervous about where we would land. The Soviet airfield was some miles outside Berlin, and we were expected at Gatow in the British Zone. That night we were to dine with General Sir Brian Robertson, who was in charge of the British Zone of Germany. Fortunately our plane was allowed to land at Gatow. The Russians' actions were the high point of hospitality, but it would have saved a lot of embarrassment if they had informed us in advance.

On arrival we had a brief conference with the leaders of the Berlin Socialists, who explained the problems of establishing the party within the Russian sector. This conference witnessed a remarkable contribution from Harold Laski. I had travelled with him many times and never found him bitter. Though he was not an orthodox Jew, he was always prepared to fight for legitimate Jewish causes. He felt keenly the suffering of his people at the Nazis' hands and believed that the German people should not escape responsibility for the havoc committed in their name.

In an emotional torrent of words Laski demanded justice and

retribution. It was a moving occasion, though I felt more than a little sorry for one or two of the Germans who had themselves spent years in Hitler's concentration camps.

* * *

Czechoslavakia

I first visited Eastern Europe in October 1945 as a fraternal delegate to the Conference of the Czechoslovakian Social Democrats. En route to Prague the British aircraft in which I was flying needed to refuel at Frankfurt, in the American Zone of Germany. Unfortunately because wartime arrangements had finished, the Americans were reluctant to supply the fuel and a protracted argument ensued. By the time the matter was settled it was too late to take off.

We asked the Americans where we could spend the night. Their first offer was a transit camp, which we did not take kindly. The British pilot explained at embarrassing length how important I was, and eventually they accommodated us at the Park Hotel in Frankfurt.

The next day we awoke to find that a thick fog had settled making take-off impossible. We succeeded in taking off on the third day but returned to Frankfurt almost immediately with engine trouble. Then the fog returned and delayed us for three further days. In the meantime I had been contacted by the members of a small military mission who were anxious to offer assistance. These British and French officers treated us so hospitably that I had great difficulty amidst a good-humoured political debate in refusing a mixture of wine and whisky. Indeed I had to hold my hand over my glass. Finally, almost a week late I flew to Prague. I had been missing for a week and no one had bothered to investigate where I was!

The main business was over, but I was able to give my fraternal delegate's speech during the mass demonstration that concluded the Conference. I also made contact with socialists from other parts of Europe who were attending in a similar capacity.

There was one amusing incident. The British Ambassador invited me to share his box at the theatre for the first night of a J. B. Priestley play. As we entered the box we saw the Union Flag draped there. The audience stood up and applauded so they must have thought I was Priestley. Anyway I sat there for three hours listening to the play performed in the Czech language. I knew most of his plays but I had not the faintest idea what this was about. I later discovered it was *Desert Highway*.

Morgan addresses Prague Conference

I spent three more days in Prague meeting my Czechoslovakian hosts. The country's Prime Minister, Zdeněk Fierlinger, was a Social Democrat but the party was in coalition with the Communists. Everyone that I met was certain that this was the only way to preserve democracy.

I discussed the situation at great length with Edvard Beneš, the co-founder and second President of Czechoslovakia. Beneš was unhappy that many of his friends in the West had criticised his action in November 1943 of signing the Czech-Soviet Alliance, which at once became the basis of the country's foreign policy. He had been hurt by the criticism and wanted people to know he had acted in the best interests of Czech democracy. He wanted to avoid any conflict between the local Social Democrats and the government-in-exile (as happened to the Poles). Such dissension would have caused unnecessary suffering and would have damaged Czech freedom. Though the Communists played an important part in the government the Socialists remained strong and independent.

Subsequent events destroyed the faith that he had invested in his policy. In February 1948, with Fierlinger's connivance, the Communists carried out a bloodless coup. Their candidates who had been defeated in the elections were installed in power by the police, under Communist direction. Five months later Dr Beneš resigned to be replaced by the Communist Klement Gottwald.

Beneš, a great European, had devoted his life to moulding a free, independent and democratic Czechoslovakia, and had tried to defend it with collective security. He strove for better understanding between Russia and the West, only to see his hopes shattered by the Allies' failure to maintain in peacetime the unity forged in war.

* * *

Germany

On the 17th June 1946 I visited the British Zone of Germany as a member of a National Council of Labour delegation, exploring the possibility of liaison with the Social Democrats, the trade unions and the co-operative movement there.

The establishment of political parties was controlled by military government orders. Permits only extended to the borders of a single *Kreis* (district) at first; later these smaller parties were allowed to amalgamate into provincial or zonal organisations. The restrictions were intended to prevent the formation of a neo-Nazi party and to avoid having too many splinter groups with no distinctive programme. Up to the time of our visit the following parties had received permits: SPD (Social Democrats), KPD (Communists), Free Democrats, Centre, Free Radical Socialists, and Conservatives.

Many in the SPD, believing that internal divisions had facilitated Hitler's rise to power, favoured an all-inclusive Workers' Party. Dr Kurt Schumacher led the opposition to this line and insisted on the establishment of an independent democratic socialist organisation. Ironically, the argument was partly resolved by the speed with which the Communists were organising their own groups.

The SPD were also alarmed by the campaign for fusion within the Russian sector of Germany, where a Socialist Unity Party had been formed under the joint leadership of the Social Democrat Otto

Grotewohl and Wilhelm Pieck the Communist. By the time we arrived, the SPD had adopted a strong line against fusion. The Social Democrats were forbidden to operate anywhere in the Russian Zone apart from East Berlin. Even there the Russian commandant refused to recognise SPD officials. Still the party was stronger than it had been during the Weimar Republic.

I could not escape feeling that the first wave of enthusiasm for democracy had already passed its peak there, as the Germans were more concerned with the immediate problem of hunger than they were with politics. Accordingly we made a strong recommendation in our report that trade unions should be established immediately, so that they could be in operation before the winter. We also stressed that young Germans should be educated in democracy. The Nazis had succeeded in divorcing Germans from any effective contact with other countries, particularly information about employment. We found the people eager to learn about British democracy, Britain's labour movement and the working conditions in the UK. We recommended that the British Zone establish information centres where a representative selection of newspapers and periodicals would be available. We also emphasised the importance of broadcasting up-to-date news and views.

After examining the policy and programme of the SPD we concluded that they were broadly in line with parties participating in the International Socialist Conference. Not all of those parties shared our opinion, but as I explained previously, the SPD was finally admitted in June 1948.

In November 1949 I was to visit Germany again, this time to convey to the SPD the terms of a resolution passed by the British Labour Party's National Executive on the subject of the dismantling of German industry. On my way there I met representatives of the French Socialists, and was delighted to find that their views coincided with ours. It remained for me to persuade the SPD to co-operate with the Allies on this matter.

When I arrived in Germany I was met by an army captain with an urgent message from General Sir Brian Robertson. Following the publication of the Petersburg Agreement there had been a bitter dispute between the Socialist Dr Schumacher and Dr Adenauer of the Christian Democrats, which resulted in Schumacher being suspended from Parliament for 20 sessions. The General was anxious to have the co-operation of both men, and he urged me to use my influence. I persuaded the Socialist leader to talk with Adenauer, and General Robertson fixed the meeting for the following evening.

To my surprise Schumacher arrived with two lawyers in tow, but the discussion went pretty smoothly, and Adenauer lifted the suspension. This story is a typical example of the tact and consideration shown by Sir Brian in handling the affairs of the British Zone of Germany.

The SPD was conducting a campaign which appeared to question the validity of the Petersburg Agreement, an entirely false position for the party to take. Having previously claimed to be the great protagonist of international co-operation, it was now aligning itself with the nationalists who wanted to retain the Ruhr. I pointed out to the German Socialists when I met them that their decision was quite disastrous. British Labour saw the Agreement as fundamentally good, both for Germany and for Europe. It would calm any French fears about security and prepare the way for a Franco-German rapprochement.

At a meeting of the SPD's Parliamentary group, Dr Schumacher made a long speech on eight specific points. I then explained the feelings of the British and French Socialists, and passed on the invitation from the French to have three-way discussions in December on the whole problem. I succeeded in getting them to accept this invitation.

Schumacher was a truly exceptional man. He had lost an arm in the First World War, his health and his eyesight were damaged irreparably by ten years in Dachau concentration camp, and his leg had to be

Morgan with Kurt Schumacher

amputated after the war, yet his spirit remained unbroken. When he died on the 20th August 1952 at the age of 56, his funeral procession filing through Hannover was a mile long, and the free world mourned his passing.

* * *

Austria and Hungary

In November 1946 I attended the Congress of the Austrian Socialist Party in Vienna at the invitation of its leader, Dr Schaerf. The city presented a grim picture. Although there was much less destruction than in most other European cities, many side streets were still filled with rubble. I saw only a few cafes and shops open, and they had little to sell. The main hotels were occupied by the Allied Forces, and the whole city was subject to strict control by the Four Powers.

Morgan with Renner and Seitz

I was warmly welcomed at the Congress and had the pleasure of meeting two venerable leaders of European socialism, Karl Renner and Karl Seitz. Renner, a man of great charm, wit and learning, had led the First Austrian Republic in 1918 and he held the same position in the Second Republic when I met him. In the intervening period, despite persecution by Dollfuss and later by the Nazis, he had been an influence for good in

119

Austria and in Europe. Seitz, the Mayor of Vienna from 1923-34, had built the world famous flats for workers. European socialism was fortunate to have two such wise and experienced counsellors in the upheaval caused by the Second World War.

The Austrians expressed their disappointment that they were not enjoying the freedom that they had anticipated after the signing in June of the new Control Agreement. They claimed that many economic difficulties were aggravated by restrictions on the traffic of goods across the zones. Nevertheless they were confident in their ability to lead the nation towards democratic socialism. This faith was ultimately rewarded despite the difficulties caused by the failure of the Allied Nations to sign the Austrian Peace Treaty until 1955. The Socialists were in coalition government from 1946 and Dr Schaerf became President of Austria.

Árpád Szakasits, the General Secretary of the Hungarian Social Democrats, also attended the Congress. At its conclusion he invited me to share his car and to visit his country. After crossing the Hungarian border we were met at various points by groups of enthusiastic party workers. In the towns, vast crowds greeted us and brass bands struck up the two countries' national anthems. One bandleader, presumably unacquainted with 'God Save the King', started the 'Marseillaise', but even so had to hum the section that the band could not manage.

Arrangements had been made for us to stop for lunch, where a great feast would be provided. It was Swine Sunday, and there were vast quantities of pork, sausage and offal. Unfortunately, although I was hungry, everything was too highly seasoned for me, and I had to watch my hosts eating. I did enjoy the beautiful pastries served as pudding.

Finally we reached Budapest. Although badly damaged during the War it appeared to have advanced further towards recovery than Vienna. New permanent bridges had been erected over the Danube, the shops were well stocked, and generally a great deal of repair work had been done. Industrial production had already reached 60% of pre-war levels despite the transfer of some machinery to the Soviet Union as an act of reparation.

The state had just emerged from an extraordinary period of inflation, during which numbers like sixtillion became commonplace. A few locals even seemed quite proud that some pengo notes needed 29 noughts to have any value. The pengo was being replaced by the forint. Stabilisation was achieved by establishing a structure of prices and wages more in keeping with the real value of the goods and services available. Workers' wages were set at 55% of their pre-war level. The policy appeared to be successful, as production was steadily increasing.

Hungary had to make reparation payments to Czechoslovakia and to the Soviet Union. The latter was also entitled to exploit certain assets previously belonging to Germany, so four Russo-Hungarian companies were established for bauxite, civil aviation, oil production and navigation of the Danube. By agreeing to import Hungarian goods, the Soviet Union could play a significant role in the country's post-war industrial development.

In a general election that was deemed free and fair by all observers, the Smallholders secured 57%, the Social Democrats 18% and the Communists 17%. These parties formed a coalition government. During my visit I spoke with the leaders of all three governing groups. The Communists had clearly misjudged their party's popularity and the extent of anti-Soviet feeling within the country. Of course the Russians would not have allowed a free election if they had realised how badly the Communist Party would fare. They made sure that this did not happen in Romania or Bulgaria.

Immediately after the Hungarian election the Communists had tried to repair the damage. They made certain demands which were sure to be rejected by the Smallholders, thus creating a crisis. The majority party eventually yielded to public pressure and gave the Communists the key post of Minister of the Interior, with control of the police and of the whole administration. The Hungarian Prime Minister in a private conversation put it simply, "I was advised to make the appointment".

After my visit the Communists put into action their plan to portray a number of the Smallholders as reactionary and unworthy to be in the coalition. Again they overestimated their power, as they only managed to get twenty members expelled: not enough to change the balance of power

However, the Communists were successful in absorbing the Social Democratic trades union into a 'Left Wing Bloc'. They next created a series of artificial crises within the coalition, leading to the collapse of the government. The new elections in August 1947 were under Soviet control and were anything but free and fair. The Communists emerged as the major party.

In June 1948, when the Communists demanded the complete absorption of the Social Democrats, the leaders lacked the willpower to resist. Only Anna Kéthly, the Deputy Speaker of Parliament, and Antal Bán, the Minister of Industry, spoke against, and they were overwhelmed at the Congress where Árpád Szakasits betrayed his party to the Communists. Antal Bán promptly left the country but Anna stayed, and though she took no further part in politics she suffered years of persecution. István Riesz, the Social Democrats' Minister for Justice, died in prison from kidney trouble – a euphemism for being beaten to death.

Szakasits was rewarded for his treachery by being made President of Hungary, but he too ended up in gaol when he was no longer useful to his masters.

The British Labour Party delegation to Moscow had heard Stalin speak about two roads to Socialism, but those words proved hollow. Those in Hungary who refused to travel the road to Communist dictatorship were liquidated or imprisoned. This constant suppression of freedom ultimately led to the Hungarian Revolution of 1956.

* * *

Romania

When I visited Romania in June 1947 the threat of famine hung over the whole nation. By this time I was convinced that Europe had to decide on united action to save the continent from sliding into famine and chaos. Romania epitomised much of Europe's tragedy and despair. Millions of workers were struggling to maintain life on wage rates and food levels that were pitifully low, and the plight of the peasants was little better.

As my colleague Sam Watson and I travelled in the royal train from Bucharest to Constanza we saw a countryside left dry and barren by three years of drought. Peasants were driving their small flocks and herds in a constant search for the few blades of grass that could mean the difference

Morgan greeted off the train by Romanian Social Democrats

between life and death. At the Port of Constanza, an elevator built for the export of grain from this once fertile area was now used solely for the import of maize from the USA to save the country from starvation.

In Bucharest the shops had had no supplies of bread for five months; it was only available on the black market. We met Moldavian peasants and their families who had wandered up to 700 miles in search of work and food – necessities denied them in their own communities by long periods of drought.

Fruit at controlled prices had disappeared from the city but could be bought by anyone with the time and the money to go out into the countryside to buy it. A suit of clothes would cost more than six months' salary. Housing standards were low, social services almost non-existent. Illiteracy was widespread, a four-year education being the norm. We spoke to a boy under thirteen who was working a twelve-hour day operating a lift in a block of flats.

I visited factories and workshops, and examined the prodigious efforts to get production going again despite the shortages of raw materials and food. Though there was no lack of manpower, output was less than half of what it had been before the war.

Many of Romania's problems were caused by the years of conflict and drought and by the decisions of past regimes. I spoke to large audiences about British social democracy, and I gained the impression that people there were eagerly seeking that same democratic freedom.

I was greatly impressed by the solidarity of the rank and file social democrats and their determination to adhere to their beliefs. However, the unsettled political situation contributed in no small measure to the distress and misery of the population. Many feared persecution and imprisonment, and we discovered that one sixth of the country's political prisoners belonged to the party. I pleaded with the authorities for their right of trial and was told that their cases would be heard as soon as possible. I was also given repeated assurances about press freedom, but the London *Times* was banned and press releases of my speeches were censored before they could be issued.

Despite every restriction on personal freedom, we met a number of men and women of great courage and integrity, qualities for which they were to suffer persecution and disgrace.

Shortly after we left, Mr Mera, the Under Secretary for Education, was convicted for a string of charges either false or ludicrous, like 'having tea with the arch-enemy of socialism Morgan Phillips'. Anna Samueli, who had translated all the speeches that I made in Romania, was given twenty

Morgan with Romanian Social Democrats

years imprisonment as an enemy of the state. I can only assume that she translated them too accurately.

* * *

Italy

The Italian Socialist Party (PSLI) was re-formed in 1944 after the fall of Mussolini but it was soon torn by dissension over policy, especially the leaders' decision to work with the Communists. Finally one group broke away completely to create a new party, Unita Socialista. By 1947 many within PSLI were pushing for reunification. The International Socialist Conference in Zurich considered a recommendation from its own commission that the two parties work together in the forthcoming Italian elections. Unfortunately a long and clever speech by Pietro Nenni, the PSLI leader, with the backing of the French veteran Salomon Grumbach, persuaded the Conference to retract the recommendation.

I visited Italy in March 1948 and had discussions with Ivan Matteo Lombardo, the Unita Secretary, as well as with Pietro Nenni, who was forming a Popular Front Alliance with the Communists.

On my return to London I sent Lombardo the following message:

> 'We in England feel the greatest satisfaction that in Italy one body of socialists at least has chosen the way of liberty and freedom'.

124

Morgan with Nenni

On the eve of the Italian election, 37 Labour MPs sent a telegram of support to Pietro Nenni. The telegram was discussed at Labour's National Executive Committee meeting a fortnight later. By that time more than half of the signatories had stated either that they had not actually signed or that they had signed under a misapprehension and wished to retract. The NEC decided to expel John Platts-Mills MP, the alleged organiser of the telegram, and to request each of the remaining signatories to undertake not to participate in any further such action. All of them gave this undertaking and the whole matter was swiftly forgotten, despite an unsuccessful attempt to revive it at Labour's Annual Conference.

On Comisco's behalf I wrote to the PSLI, warning that it would be excluded from the International Socialist Conference if it continued to co-operate 'with a party which obeys the directives and purposes of the Cominform'. Riccardo Lombardi gave the party's reply in a letter published in the PSLI's newspaper *Avanti*. After calling me a clown and a self-styled pope or king, he hailed the 'pact of unity of action with the Communist Party as being within the scope of the Italian working-class struggle and the defence of democracy in our country. Morgan Phillips cares only about getting our party to change fronts and to pass over to the anti-Communist and anti-Soviet alignment'.

From December 1949 the PSLI was excluded from the International Conference and replaced by Unita Socialista, but seven years later it appeared that the breach between the two parties could be healed at last. The brutal Soviet suppression of Hungary coming so soon after Khrushchev's denunciation of Stalin gave Nenni second thoughts about his alliance with the Communists. He was seriously contemplating a merger with the Unita Party led by Giuseppe Saragat.

After receiving a long letter from Signor Saragat, the Socialist International agreed to send a three-man team to Italy to assist the fusion of the two parties. I was on the team, together with the Austrian Vice Chancellor Schaerf and Pierre Commin, the Assistant Secretary of the French Socialists. In this connection Pierre Commin and I were invited to Nenni's Party Congress from the 6th-10th February 1957, where reunification of the two groups was on the agenda. The British Labour Party sent a fraternal delegate, my friend and colleague Nye Bevan MP, and Richard Crossman MP attended in his capacity as a journalist.

At the start of the Congress Nenni made a three-hour speech advocating socialist unity and a break with Communism. He and the speakers that followed him showed their deep shock at the aftermath of the Hungarian Revolution. However, the elections for the party's central committee gave increased power to the pro-Communist Rodolfo Morandi faction. Nenni offered to resign but after prolonged negotiations he stayed as Secretary and Leader.

Bevan, Crossman and I then went to Rome to meet Giuseppe Saragat, the leader of Unita. In our discussions he seemed in favour of a merger, but subsequently he made little effort because of pressure from his own officials, who feared losing their positions. The move towards unity of these two socialists, men of integrity and courage, were constantly frustrated by people in their own parties.

* * *

Yugoslavia
Alliance of Tito Clique and right-wing socialist traitors
Headline in the English language Soviet journal 'For a Lasting Peace For People's Democracy'

In September 1950, Yugoslavia, no longer part of the Soviet bloc, was anxious for political and economic co-operation with the West. I was part of a three-man Labour British delegation invited to visit the country. My colleagues were Sam Watson, the Party Chairman, and Harry Earnshaw, a member of our National Executive. The entire executive committee of the People's Front, Yugoslavia's ruling party, met us at the airport

The country had experienced a very difficult time after breaking away from the Cominform (the organisation coordinating Communist parties under Soviet direction) in June 1948. The Soviet Union had been conducting an extensive blockade to starve Yugoslavia into surrender, and a severe drought just before my visit caused further deprivation. Coffee, soap and other basics were extremely scarce and consumer goods like toothbrushes, razor blades, needles and pencils were practically unobtainable. While the average wage was £7 a week, butter had increased in price from £2 to £3 per lb, sugar and lard from £1 to £2 10 shillings per lb, and coffee (when available) from £3-£4 to £10 per lb. Potatoes cost six times more than previously.

Despite the hardships, everywhere we went we found genuine enthusiasm for the regime. Though some of this was simulated for our benefit, I did notice a real contrast with the Soviet Union. The Yugoslavs seemed eager to talk about current affairs and there was far more opportunity for the individual to participate in local politics.

Strenuous efforts were being made to develop heavy and light industries in order to produce tractors, harvesters, electric generating plants and some consumer goods, but it was not easy to create a highly skilled, industrialised working class in a short space of time. The directors of some enterprises listed their qualifications in this order: 1. Wartime service as partisan; 2. Membership of the Communist Party; 3. Previous relevant experience.

We visited a textile factory at Novi Sad and watched the election of the works council which would run it. The process was complicated but secret and manifestly fair. Under recent legislation each factory had a works council with an executive committee that met regularly with the director to plan the work of the factory. Although the director was chosen by the state, the works council could seek his removal. Responsibility was thus devolved to those actively occupied in the industry.

One of our visits was to a local gaol where, unhindered, we spoke with political prisoners. I asked the governor why his establishment was not run by a workers' council. He replied with a wry smile that none of the inmates were serving less than ten years.

In local government too Yugoslavia lacked the Russian level of bureaucracy, but it was still a one party, police state. The most important instrument of supervision of government was the Popular Front, which represented about 75% of the voters. While essentially a political organisation it included people who for religious or other reasons could not join the Communist Party. There was no opportunity to develop alternative parties. While we were in the country, Dusan Brkic, the Croatian Vice Premier, and fourteen other leading party members were suspended and placed under surveillance for alleged pro-Soviet activities.

We began our visit with two days of discussions, lasting 14 hours, with seven leading politicians including Dr Neskovic, the national leader of the People's Front, and we were staggered by the complete frankness of their responses. It was a straight, honest, cards-on-the-table discussion. This could not have happened in Russia. During our meetings the Yugoslavs argued openly among themselves and contradicted each other. In Moscow in 1946 everyone we met below the rank of Stalin told us, 'We're sorry, we are not authorised to talk politics'. In Yugoslavia people seemed not only free but anxious to talk.

Particularly impressive was Milovan Djilas, the senior member of President Tito's politburo, who spoke openly about the defects of Soviet Communism. This was only a short time after Yugoslavia's break with the Cominform, and Tito's rejoinders to Stalin's denunciations had been so restrained that a reconciliation was possible. Djilas destroyed that illusion completely. Not only did he hit ruthlessly at the Russian centralism but also he showed obvious enthusiasm for the importation of a more truly democratic system. The Iron Curtain had divided the world into two camps. The line-up for the next conflict seemed complete – and then came the great rift between Tito and Stalin, for which Djilas had clearly been the inspiration. As he described it:

> 'The people heeded us when we called on them to fight in the war for independence. They made enormous sacrifices. We have no right to betray them with weasel words about becoming the leading power in the world of socialism and about socialist solidarity with the Russians'.

He fervently believed that democracy was possible in Yugoslavia's one party state. After all, capitalism did not interfere with democracy so long as it did not endanger the capitalist ownership of the means of production: As he put it:

> 'I do not see why this battle of opinion should not develop in our own country on the basis of socialist ownership.'

The level of Yugoslav hospitality was embarrassing. In many places we were greeted with cries of 'Long live Phillips', 'Long live Watson' and 'Long Live Earnshaw'. We stayed at the villa of a government minister

The delegation and their Yugoslav hosts

on the outskirts of Belgrade and were attended by numerous servants including 'Chico', the headwaiter of the city's biggest hotel. One morning we unwisely asked him for bacon and eggs. He presented us with masses of ham and six eggs each in a country where eggs were an expensive luxury.

We were invited to meet President Tito at his villa outside Belgrade. He received us in his capacious study, which contained a heavy desk, a chess table, a sizable relief map of Yugoslavia, a bust of Lenin and a massive oil painting, a gift from the Croatian Republic. The painting, which hung on a wall behind his desk, depicted a dramatic scene from the Croatian Peasants' Revolt in 1573, and revealed his pride in Yugoslavia's freedom.

Tito sat at his desk, speaking to us through an interpreter and smoking cigarettes through a pipe-shaped holder, which he was rarely seen without. Though he had learnt some English in Lepoglava prison – enough to be able to correct his interpreter from time to time – he rarely spoke the language.

When I asked how he had come to invite us to Yugoslavia, he instantly replied that that the invitation was part of his open-door policy towards progressive thinkers, and that he considered the Labour Party the greatest organisation of workers in Europe. We would be among the best able to understand the social revolution taking place in his country. Though he did not minimise the economic difficulties he was confident that with a little outside help his people would not starve during the coming winter.

Much as he desired better relations with Europe and America, Tito declared with characteristic forcefulness that he had no more wish to become part of the Western bloc than to go back cap in hand to the Cominform.

Our discussions became less serious and Tito chatted about soccer and baseball. He knew all about the New York Giants and the Brooklyn Dodgers. He also enquired after the playwright George Bernard Shaw and asked us to convey his greetings to 'that great socialist genius'.

Tito and Morgan Phillips

At one point we were alarmed by an enormous wolfhound which charged into the room, but Tito explained that 'Tiger' was his special pet. In 1943, when he was leading the Partisans, a German bomber plane had made a surprise attack. As everyone hit the ground a bomb exploded, killing many of the Yugoslavs. Tito was injured but escaped death because his dog was deliberately covering him. He never forgot that his pet had died to save him, and in return he rescued a German dog and adopted him. He and Tiger became inseparable.

Among the exhibits in the President's villa was a collection of miners' lamps from all over the world. There was no British lamp – a gap which Sam Watson, the Durham Miners' leader, promised to fill as soon as he returned to England.

Two years later I had a personal invitation from Marshal Tito to bring my wife, son and daughter to Yugoslavia for a holiday. I gladly accepted and enjoyed one of the pleasantest vacations of my life, not least because my wife did all the sightseeing, which is an unavoidable part of visiting a new state, while I relaxed at the comfortable villa at Opatija.

Morgan relaxes by the sea

In 1954 it was reported that Milovan Djilas, Tito's senior adviser, had been suddenly removed from office. He was learning the hard way that Communism suffered no 'battle of opinion'.

After a staged trial his pension was taken away and his family victimised. People who contacted him were immediately interrogated by the police and given the choice of staying away from him or becoming informers. There were constant attempts to provoke him and his wife into physical retaliation. When a woman (presumably an agent) attacked his wife Stefania in the street he took the assailant to court. Although she was fined for the assault, Djilas was ordered to move to a residence that was not even completed. When he wrote to me about all this I decided to send a private letter in a purely personal capacity to Marshal Tito:

'My Dear Marshal

It is indeed painful to me to have to write a letter of this kind because since my visit to you six years ago I have been particularly interested in the experiments in your country and have become attached to you and your colleagues.

I have appreciated the nature and the extent of the problems that you have had to overcome but recently I have been disturbed by news that I have received. I have no doubt that you are aware when you put Djilas and Dedijer on trial Mr Sam Watson and I had a private and informal talk with your ambassador in London. At that time we made our view clear that this was a kind of test that would demonstrate to progressive opinion throughout the world the measure of your progress towards a real socialist democracy.

We were relieved at the result of the trial but now we find that as a result of evidence that has been accumulated over the last eighteen months our relief was a little misplaced.

I understand for example that you have deprived Mr Djilas of his war pension and that you have dismissed members of his family from their jobs. This was extended even to the husband of one of Mr Djilas's sisters. Even more distant relatives have been dismissed without any rights from the army after long service because they visited his family.

I appreciate that Djilas is a political journalist and that in a country such as yours with the publications you have he is unable to earn a livelihood in that field but I should have thought that some means could have been found to enable him to earn an honourable livelihood. Not only is his livelihood affected but I understand that he has been moved from his villa into a flat and that he is now to be dispossessed of that because it is argued that he has no right to a separate workroom because he is not an intellectual.

The same kind of story is equally true of Colonel Jovan Barovic, and I am told there are a number of people who have been given court sentences because they have shown sympathy to someone who is a former comrade in the struggle for the liberation of Yugoslavia.

Furthermore your secret police have extended their activities; they photograph and follow around your former comrade and indeed according to my evidence they make no secret of the fact that this is what they are doing.

I must confess that I am appalled that the country which in 1950 I supported in articles and public speeches and in private documents to the then Foreign Secretary of our own Government Ernest Bevin should have slipped back into the evil ways of the Cominform countries. I do not know whether this is related to what appears to be a shift in the foreign policy of your country – that however is not my business. I am only concerned with the human aspect of administration and I still hope that you can in your relations with individuals demonstrate to the world the fundamental superiority of a socialist system of society. I do not want to say anything publicly in this matter yet but I shall be very glad to receive your observations'.

I received no reply from the Marshal, who clearly passed the letter on to the party newspaper *Borba*. On the 20th May 1956 it published a savage attack on me by Veljko Vlahovi , the President of the Foreign Relations Commission of the Socialist Alliance of the Working People of Yugoslavia. Inevitably I was charged with interfering in the internal affairs of another country and of showing 'a hopeless apathy and helpless resignation' towards worse things happening within the British sphere of control, such as Kenya and Cyprus.

When the Hungarian people made their brave stand later that year, Yugoslavia abstained from a UN vote to put the Soviet intervention on the agenda. Djilas, in a statement to the French Press Agency, criticised his government for the 'abandonment of the principles of sovereignty and of the right of every nation to develop its own internal affairs'. His arrest, his secret trial for activities against the regime and his imprisonment followed swiftly. Despite my efforts and those of many others to secure his release he remained in gaol for the whole three years of his sentence.

The story of Milovan Djilas, intellectual revolutionary, communist leader, unorthodox theoretician and finally scapegoat, sums up the modern dilemma. Men of good will from all classes of society have supported the establishment of communist regimes in many countries in the sincere belief that a free and democratic society would eventually emerge. Djilas was not the first who failed to find the road back from communism to a free society.

Methodism not Marxism

In the United Kingdom General Election of February 1950 Labour secured over 13 million votes, more than ever before and representing over half of the total poll. However a major reorganisation of the constituencies meant that the Government's majority tumbled from 146 to just five. Clearly, another General Election would soon be needed to achieve a Government with a working majority.

Because of my role as Comisco's Chairman and Permanent British Representative I met a great many European socialists. I became more and more aware of the extent to which it was believed, particularly among the old guard, that one could not be a socialist without being a Marxist. This I regarded as an obsolete idea, particularly in light of the evidence from the British Labour Movement, and it might harm our chances in a future General Election if the Tories could portray us as a revolutionary Marxist party. With both considerations in mind I decided to address the International Conference in Copenhagen in June 1950. I was unprepared for the controversy that my speech on 'Marxism and the Labour Party' aroused.

The full text is given in an appendix to this book, so I will reproduce only some of the points that I made:

> 'British socialism owes little to Karl Marx either in theory or practice or in its methods of organising the working class. Trotsky was not far wrong when he said that that the English Revolution brought about by the Puritans was nourished on Biblical texts, the French Revolution on the abstractions of democracy and the Russian Revolution on Marxism... Marx's conception of the political organisation required for the waging of the class war was not accepted by the British Labour Movement. British socialism has pointed the way to the achievement of that rarest phenomenon in history – a revolutionary change in political control and class relations without physical conflict'.

Later on, while describing the antecedents of the British Labour movement, I made some remarks that really caught the public imagination and led to my address being dubbed the 'Methodism not Marxism' speech, a phrase first coined by the London *Times*, though it was Ian Mackay of the *News Chronicle* whose report made the biggest impact:

> 'Methods of religious organisation arising out of the evangelical revival of the 18th Century were incorporated in the organisation of the radical societies, the political associations, the trade unions and the friendly societies which throve apace in the 19th Century. When Chartism revived after its defeat in 1839 its

reorganisation as a national movement owed a good deal to radicals and democrats who belonged to the Methodist Church'.

In the debate that followed, the delegates tried to find a sufficient measure of agreement on the fundamental principles of socialism to warrant the re-establishment of the Socialist International. Comisco then set to work preparing a resolution that would achieve this aim.

On the 5th January 1951 Victor Larock, a leading Belgian Socialist, wrote an open letter to me as Chairman of Comisco in his newspaper *Le Peuple* expressing his party's unanimous desire for the formal re-institution of the Socialist International. The French Socialists also published his letter and indicated their support. The Dutch Labour paper *Het Vrije Volk* was more cautious, realising that the British would not accept a supranational authority: 'We do not see how an International could give better service than Comisco does at present and we might raise expectations that we cannot fulfil'.

On the 24th January the British Labour Party National Executive endorsed Victor Larock's sentiments provided that the International's decisions should not be binding on all constituent parties. The Comisco meeting on the 3rd March, with the distinguished French Socialist Louis Levy deputising for me in the Chair, agreed on the terms of a resolution to permit the re-establishment of the International. It included this paragraph:

> 'Socialist co-operation must be based on consent. The resolutions passed by an international socialist body must reflect agreement freely reached. They cannot constitute a binding command on parties which are individually responsible to their own members and to a national electorate. An international body cannot claim mandatory powers'.

The 8th International Socialist Conference, held in Frankfurt-am-Main from the 30th June to the 3rd July 1951, approved the Comisco resolution by a show of hands. Thereupon four Red Falcons (young German Social Democrats), two girls and two boys, advanced on the platform with a great scarlet banner, on which the words *Socialist International* were emblazoned in gold. Erich Ollenhauer, the Conference Chairman, presented this beautiful banner to me as Chairman of Comisco. The Conference had become the First Congress of the Socialist International.

After singing the 'Internationale', the delegates went on to discuss a 3000-word statement of 'The Aims and Tasks of Democratic Socialism', with four supplementary statements on political democracy, economic democracy, international democracy and cultural progress. It ended:

> 'Finally it is recognised that no nation can solve all its economic and social problems in isolation. Absolute national sovereignty must be transcended. Democratic socialists recognise the maintenance of world peace as the supreme task in our time'.

I spoke about world socialist action in the struggle for peace:

> 'The first task we all face is to take the military measures necessary to deter any aggression that might start a Third World War. That catastrophe can be prevented only by rearmament up to a level high enough to deter the rulers in the Kremlin from repeating their gamble somewhere else'.

I reminded those socialists still obsessed by doctrinal suspicions of the USA:

> 'The United States of America, whose failure to support the League of Nations helped to make the Second World War inevitable, has today shown itself in the forefront of the free democracies in its devotion to peace and in its readiness to sacrifice for peace'.

Despite the fears raised by the conflict in Korea I felt it was a time for optimism:

> 'I take this opportunity of declaring on behalf of my party, and I hope of us all, my faith in the ability of socialism to meet the challenge of the modern world. We socialists cannot claim a monopoly of wisdom or of moral strength. We must approach the formidable problems which await us with genuine humility. But we can approach them also with a sober confidence. As socialists we draw our inspiration from the same moral sources as have inspired movements for freedom, progress and justice throughout history. To this deep moral purpose we can add a scientific understanding of the political and economic forces which shape the modern world. This combination is irresistible – providing we work together and keep our eyes fixed steadfastly to our goal: a world of plenty, peace and freedom. We shall not fail this responsibility'.

Needless to say, some delegates felt that the statements did not go far enough, especially those from countries like Germany and Japan, which could attribute many of their misfortunes to capitalism. As Kurt Schumacher had said when he welcomed the delegates to his country:

> 'The big property owners are trying to persuade the world that freedom is dependent upon if not identical with a free market economy... In the fight against Soviet totalitarianism great damage is done through the attempt to identify liberal capitalism with democracy. A policy of reaction and social injustice is no basis for a modern democratic state struggling against dictatorship'.

All of the statements were endorsed by the delegates.

On the final day of the Conference the Belgian Victor Larock reported on a Council meeting held the previous evening to choose the officials for the Socialist International:

> 'Morgan Phillips has been elected Chairman in recognition of his position in the Labour Party, of the great achievements of that party and of the responsible part he has played in building up Comisco. He has fulfilled his tasks as Chairman in Comisco with perfect impartiality, always conscious of his international obligations which he is clearly able to keep distinct from his national responsibilities. He can also be relied on to judge any issue on the basis of the facts and to insist that those facts be established'.

Louis Levy of the French Socialists and Erich Ollenhauer from Germany were elected Vice-Chairmen, and Julius Braunthal Secretary. As Victor said of Julius:

> 'All parties know with what devotion and zeal he has discharged his duties as Administrative Secretary of Comisco'.

I was a proud man when these appointments were approved by the delegates.

* * *

Anna Kéthly

I have described how Anna Kéthly stayed on in Hungary after her brave but doomed fight against a communist takeover of her party. Though she took no further part in Hungarian politics she was arrested on the 14th June 1950 on the government's orders, and subsequently sentenced at a secret court-martial to fifteen years in prison. When I learned of this some months later I sent an open letter to Mátyás Rákosi, the communist dictator, on the 14th April 1951:

> 'Sir,
> It has been widely reported that at a secret court-martial recently held in Budapest, Anna Kéthly, together with a number of other leading Hungarian Social Democrats, was sentenced to fifteen years' hard labour on charges of espionage for foreign powers.
> These reports have not been denied by the Hungarian Government. On behalf of Democratic Socialists all over the world I ask you to state publicly whether or not this report is true.

Anna Kéthly is famous throughout the world as a leading member of the Hungarian Workers' Movement. She was a Member of Parliament for 24 years and Deputy Speaker from 1947-1948. Her valiant resistance to the Horthy Government and the Nazi invaders made her one of the most popular of all Hungarian democratic leaders. In meetings of the International Conference since 1945 she won respect for her great integrity of character, and affection for her warmth of personality.

After the fusion of the Social Democratic Party with the Communist Party she retired from political life and lived in complete seclusion in her home. She felt nevertheless that her place was with the Hungarian working class, and she refused every suggestion by yourself that she should leave the country.

She was arrested on the 14th June 1950 together with five hundred leading Social Democrats and imprisoned without any charge being levelled against her.

If the reports I have referred to are true she has now been held for more than nine months in prison without a trial. If the report is true she has been given a life sentence, as she is already sixty-two years of age.

You yourself know from personal experience what it is to be a political prisoner. You owe your life to intervention by democratic socialists when the Horthy regime in Hungary had sentenced you to death. You know that in 1926 the Socialist International protested against your imprisonment, stating that 'the workers of all countries recognise in the methods adopted against the accused in the trial of Rákosi a policy of unjustifiable cruelty and of conscious provocation'. You know that money was collected for your defence by foreign socialists and that a young English lawyer, now a Labour MP, appeared publicly on your behalf in Budapest.

I therefore appeal to you to give Anna Kéthly at least the same opportunity as the Horthy dictatorship afforded to yourself – a public trial with independent lawyers for the defence.

At the present time the methods you have adopted compare unfavourably with those of a reactionary dictatorship before the war. I would be relieved to learn that this comparison is less than justified.'

Needless to say I received no reply. The first Congress of the new Socialist International issued an appeal 'to world public opinion no less than to all socialist parties to continue their efforts to secure a fair public trial with independent counsels for the defence. For Anna Kéthly stood for principles of freedom'.

She was not released until October 1954 after I had spoken personally to Mr Molotov, the Soviet Foreign Minister.

This was not my first brush with Rákosi. In October 1950, when he was Deputy Prime Minister, he wrote a report for the Central Committee of his party, accusing the British Labour Party of organising Hungarian Social Democrats to act as spies for British and American Intelligence. I was on the list of 'imperialist agents', together with MPs Denis Healey, Konni Zilliacus and Manny Shinwell. The latter was supposed to have thanked a delegation of Social Democrats in 1945 for aiding the espionage services during the war.

For some reason this story particularly annoyed me though it was mild compared with a lot of communist propaganda. I issued a public statement that although no such delegation had visited Britain in 1945, the Social Democrats had certainly played a leading part in the fight against German and Hungarian fascism 'at a time when Mr Rákosi was living comfortably in Russian hotels.'

'The present attack on the British Labour Party' I continued, 'is of course part of a carefully planned campaign to destroy the faith of the Hungarian workers in democratic socialism. Measures of oppression cannot destroy a movement that is rooted firmly in the minds of the Hungarian working class. A movement that survived Horthy will survive Rákosi. When the time of reckoning comes, those responsible for crimes against the Hungarian workers will not escape punishment'.

* * *

Belgium and Holland

On Monday the 27th May 1951 I had the privilege of paying an 80th year birthday tribute to Camille Huysmans, the pioneer of Belgian socialism, during the celebrations held in the Antwerp marketplace. It was unforgettable to watch 100,000 socialists from all over Belgium marching past this great man. Of course he was a figure of more than national importance. He was Secretary of the Socialist International from 1905 to 1920, and was elected President of the Labour and Socialist International (the LSI) in 1940. For fifty years, which included two world wars, he worked untiringly for the cause of international socialism. As I said in my tribute that day,

'Few men have done more to give practical effect to the idea of working class solidarity. A lifelong militant socialist, he has been continuously active in the political life of his country, entering passionately into all the problems and controversies of his day'.

Belgium also supplied another president of the LSI, Louis de Brouckère, who held the office in the crucial years between 1936 and 1939. Louis, a former professor at Brussels University, was one of the best-loved figures in the continental socialist movement, and before he died in 1951 at the age of 81 he made a great contribution to the reconstruction of the Socialist International.

Among the younger politicians I must mention my friends Eduard Anseele and Victor Larock. Eduard, coming from a notable Ghent family, was Burgomaster of that town after the Liberation in 1944 and later spent five years as Minister of Communications, before becoming Vice-President of his party. Victor, once a Professor at the Institut des Hautes Études in Ghent, held three important ministries in Belgium and then became President of the European Economic Community. Both men have striven continuously on behalf of the Socialist International.

On the 19th July 1955 Koos Vorrink, who had led the Dutch Labour Party for 21 years, died in Amsterdam aged 64. During the war he had been an active member of the Resistance and had spent three years in various concentration camps.

He was an extraordinarily gifted orator, who could hold the attention of large audiences for long periods of time. I remember attending a Conference of the Dutch Party held in the grounds of a zoo in The Hague. Koos spoke for three hours and despite the length of his speech and the noise from the animals the audience was under his spell throughout.

Two years after his death the Dutch Labour Party lost another great man, Johan Albarda. Before the war he had been President of the Parliamentary Party for fifteen years and in 1939 he succeeded Louis de Brouckère as LSI President. He spent the war years in London, serving the Dutch Government-in-exile as Minister of Public Works, Air and Transport. He took a particularly lively interest in the preparations for a new Socialist International.

✳ ✳ ✳

The International takes shape

Seven parties in exile applied for membership of the new Socialist International, those of Latvia, Lithuania, Georgia, Armenia and the Ukraine, and the Menshevik and the Socialist Party of Estonia. Though fully appreciating the hardships suffered by these groups, the British Labour Party feared that if they joined the International it might begin to seem like a conspiratorial anti-Soviet body. Consequently, when the Socialist International discussed their applications at Milan in October

1952 Clem Attlee, the British delegate, opposed acceptance.

The matter was referred to a meeting of the Bureau, as Comisco was now called, and I took the same stand as Clem. Only Denmark and Israel supported me but in deference to our views the Bureau decided that these exile parties should not have a vote in the Conference, although they had the right to speak.

Now that the Socialist International had finally come into being, we felt it imperative to make immediate contacts with socialist parties outside Europe, particularly those in the new Asian democracies. Such contacts would be to our benefit as well as to theirs, as I had pointed out in a speech to the Swedish Social Democrats on the 2nd July 1952 in Sweden:

> 'I believe that we Europeans have as much to learn from the socialists of Africa and Asia as they have to learn from us. I welcome the fact that some of them are already associated with us, for it is clear that the future of world peace and prosperity depends upon our applying in international affairs the same socialist principles as we apply to the domestic affairs of our own countries'.

The Asian parties were already trying to form their own group. Early in 1953 at a Rangoon meeting attended by delegates from Burma, India, Pakistan, Israel, the Lebanon and Japan, a permanent organisation was established with its own secretariat and with its headquarters in Rangoon. They quickly made contact with the International and sent delegates to the Congress in July 1953. These delegates invited me to attend the Bureau meeting of the Asian Socialist Conference in Hyderabad a month later.

The meeting was held in the Fort Hill Palace, as if to symbolise the great changes taking place in Asia. I was deeply impressed to observe that the business was conducted in one language, English, whereas the Congress of the Socialist International was usually conducted in English, French, German and Swedish.

Two issues dominated the meeting: peace in Asia and the struggle against colonialism. There was a general desire for the neutrality of Korea and Japan despite a sharp difference of opinion between the right-wing and the left-wing Japanese Socialist Parties.

The delegate from Indonesia, Mr Wijono, who had attended the Socialist International Conference, claimed that European socialists were not genuine in their antipathy to colonialism. He acknowledged the International's anti-colonial outlook but claimed they lacked the courage to take a clear stand against colonialism. The International had merely referred the proposed campaign to Comisco. When I was invited to speak I stressed the common ideals and principles that Europeans shared with their Asian counterparts, including the distaste for imperialism. The actions of the 1945 British Labour Government proved this. The referral to Comisco did not imply rejection. If feasible, the proposal would be accepted.

To my delight the delegates approved a five-point plan 'to secure the closest possible co-operation between the Socialist International and the Asian Socialist Conference'. The meeting was an exhilarating experience. The participants were young men, many of whom were holding ministerial or other responsible offices in their own countries. All had a profound belief in the principles of social democracy and were opposed to every form of totalitarianism.

After the meeting I had private talks with members of the Indian Socialist Party, who described to me the difficulties that they were having in bringing people to believe that democratic socialism was the only constructive way to achieve social justice and prosperity.

From India I flew on the Comet to Rangoon, where I was welcomed by a group of Burmese socialist ministers and trade unionists. Despite the machinations of the communists and the marauding raids of Chinese Nationalists, the coalition government had done much to ease the lot of the people. It had nationalised big industrial enterprises, distributed land to farmers and introduced a labour welfare scheme, educational reforms and a national health council. My visits to temporary and permanent housing and to the overcrowded university buildings convinced me of the determined way in which the Burmese were tackling their domestic problems.

Next I moved to Bangkok, the capital of Thailand, and found myself in an entirely different world. The city was surrounded by rich paddy fields separated by canals, which served every purpose from personal washing to watering of the bullocks used in the fields and on the roads. The local politicians were easygoing characters with a wonderful sense of humour but little inclination for action. They tried to convince me that the people, who were still under the tutelage system, had no revolutionary fervour because they had full bellies.

The People's Republic of China

At the Labour Party Conference in September 1953 a resolution was carried urging that 'a mission of goodwill be sent to the Soviet Union and the People's Republic of China by the Labour Party as a step forward to more friendly relations between East and West'. Consequently approaches were made to the Chinese Government.

We did not receive an answer until the following April, when permission was granted for us to send a delegation. I wrote a letter of thanks to Chou En-lai, the Chinese Premier. Shortly afterwards he visited Europe for the Geneva Conference of 1954 and expressed a wish to meet me there. He agreed to have part of our discussion recorded by the BBC.

The white and gold drawing room of the Villa Mont Fleury near Geneva was the setting for my discussion with Chou En-lai. The walls were lined with glass cabinets of fine porcelain and the carpets bore an exquisitely beautiful floral design, but the room was dominated by a massive portrait of Mao Tse Tung. This was my first acquaintance with China old and new.

The Chinese Premier hurried in wearing his plain blue-grey uniform, greeted me in Chinese and told me through an interpreter how excited he was to have just seen Charlie Chaplin in the flesh. As I was also a great fan, we began to discuss our favourite Chaplin films. Unfortunately time was pressing, and we had to move on to more serious matters.

We considered possible subjects for the BBC programme, and Chou indicated that he was not interested in the purely theoretical. 'Let's be practical', he insisted. I took him at his word and presented specific problems. He spoke of the importance that he attached to developing and expanding industrial and commercial connections with Britain, which would be to the benefit of both countries. When I asked about peace in Asia he replied that it depended on measures taken for collective security, like the Joint Statements between China and India and between China and Burma.

At the request of the Labour leader Clem Attlee I raised the issue of two American journalists imprisoned in China for 'intruding into Chinese territorial waters'. He assured me that the case would soon be cleared up (they were released shortly afterwards). I was tremendously impressed by Chou En-lai and looked forward all the more to our forthcoming trip to China.

Whilst in Geneva I discussed the arrangements for journalists who wanted to report on the tour. The Chinese authorities agreed to grant visas to six British journalists and to four from the Commonwealth, as well as to a Reuters correspondent.

We were invited to have twenty people on our delegation but that would have been too expensive for our party to fund. A smaller number was agreed and the names were chosen by lot. On the 9th August 1954 the Labour Party delegation left London Airport. I travelled with Clem Attlee, Edith Summerskill, Nye Bevan and three trade unionists, Sam Watson, Harry Earnshaw and Henry Franklin.

I bought my first camera, a Rolleiflex, so that I could later publish an illustrated account of the trip, *East Meets West.*

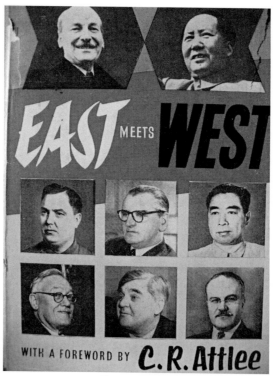

East Meets West

After spending two days in Moscow we flew on to China. On arrival in Peking I discussed with the representative of the People's Institute of Foreign Affairs whether the journalists could be given the same facilities as ourselves to visit institutions and workplaces and to speak to

Dr Edith Summerskill at the Temple of Heaven in Peking

government officials. We agreed that they should be invited to all social functions in our honour. This agreement was carried out to the letter by the Chinese authorities.

We began an extensive and gruelling sightseeing tour, visiting shops in Peking, a housing estate in Mukden, Manchuria, a collective farm in Kaokan, the steel works in Anshan and the coal mines in Kailan. The tour gave us some idea of the efforts made by the Chinese to increase agricultural and industrial production and to feed and clothe the ever-growing population.

In the Mukden housing estate I noticed that the flats – consisting of a sitting room and a bedroom – were constructed in pairs with one front door, one kitchen and one lavatory to each pair. For the average Chinese family this was very limited accommodation, but eventually it was hoped to convert the pair into one four-roomed flat. Here, as in all the living quarters that we saw, even the Peking slums, everything was scrupulously neat and clean.

The new government was not only trying to raise living standards. There was a deliberate effort to create a new morality. We learnt something of this from the British businessmen in Shanghai, who had stayed in China after the revolution despite all the difficulties involved.

145

One factory manager told me that in the past the company had lost between three and four per cent of its production to pilferers, but under the new regime they rarely lost anything. Another said that before the revolution his wife had been attacked in the street, but now she felt free to move around in any part of the city after dark completely without fear.

The marriage laws had also been changed. Marriage by arrangement was forbidden, divorce was allowed between consenting parties and widows could remarry without any social sigma.

In Peking we were able to meet the leaders of the state, including Mao Tse-tung. To be honest we were surprised to see him, as he made few public appearances and there were rumours about ill health. We found him sunburnt and fit, in good health and humour. Our discussions were frank and outspoken. The Chinese were proud of their dialectical materialism and eager to carry out the aims of the revolution. They were determined to regain the offshore islands and bitterly resented the attitude of the Western nations, particularly the USA, on this issue.

A press conference was arranged in Canton just prior to our departure for Hong Kong. I received a delegation of three British pressmen asking if I could bring the conference forward to the previous evening to allow

Chou En-lai with the Labour delegation

146

reports to appear in the morning papers in Britain. Accordingly, the conference was brought forward, even though it meant that there was insufficient time for our statement to be translated into Chinese versions. Unforgivably the British journalists mocked their Chinese counterparts for asking questions that were answered in the statement.

I formed many impressions of China and its people during the trip, but perhaps the most striking of all was the remarkable character of Chou En-lai, a world statesman.

* * *

The new rulers of Russia

In August 1954, en route for Peking, the Labour Party delegation was invited to spend two days in Moscow. As we drove from the airport to the city I was astonished by the changes that had taken place since my last visit in 1946. The roads had been widened, the volume of traffic was much heavier and there were many new skyscrapers.

Harry Earnshaw, Nye Bevan and Henry Franklin at the Lenin Memorial

On our first evening we were taken to Maxim Gorky House, 22 miles outside Moscow, to meet the man who now ruled the Soviet Union after Stalin's death, Malenkov. With him were Molotov, the Foreign Secretary, Mikoyan, Minister of Foreign Trade, and Khrushchev, First Secretary of the Communist Party. The atmosphere was cordial, the discussions candid, and I was able to form some personal impressions of the four leaders.

Malenkov was shorter than I imagined and showed a warm personality. In discussion he displayed great shrewdness and his interventions were always to the point. In addition he had a pronounced sense of humour. Molotov was his usual impeccable, inscrutable self but he was clearly worried about the emergence of China as a world power. When I managed to have a private word with him I urged him to secure the release of Anna Kéthly, who had been unjustly held in a Hungarian prison for four years. He made no promises, but she was released before the year was out.

Khrushchev, Malenkov's brother-in-law, was regarded as a vigorous bureaucrat, devoted to the party machine, and ruthless when dealing with dissenters (I am occasionally characterised the same way). This time he was in an affable mood but he left us in no doubt about his strength of will. I noted at the time:

'If, as rumour has it, the dictatorship is now shared by three or four men, I feel sure that Khrushchev is not only among their number but has a powerful voice in their decisions'. (*East Meets West*)

Two years later Khrushchev paid an official visit to Great Britain with Marshal Bulganin. By that time Malenkov, Mikoyan and Molotov had been relegated to the sidelines.

On Monday 23rd April 1956 the Labour Party gave the visitors a dinner in the Harcourt Room of the House of Commons. When they arrived they had a quick discussion, after which the Russian Ambassador told me that Marshal Bulganin would be the spokesman for the evening.

We were delighted by the Marshal's brief and friendly address. He poked fun at the protocol of the British Foreign Office:

'We would have been glad to visit some other institutions besides Downing Street. We would have been glad to visit working class districts, workers' flats. As a matter of fact we would have been glad to visit your homes.'

'You can come to my house,' smiled George Brown.

'They won't let me go,' Bulganin replied, 'Their representative of protocol will show up at some definite hour and take me back to the hotel.'

After the Marshal had finished, some diners called on Khrushchev to say a few words. He rose and unexpectedly launched into a lengthy, disjointed and often provocative address. It began promisingly:

> 'We could have closer contact with you than the ones we have now, which are as a matter of fact non-existent. Of course there is a great difference between us in political views. I am not inviting you to take up Marxism because I am sure you would be very poor Marxists – and we would be awful Labour Party members.'

However, after quoting a Russian proverb ('One may eat a man's bread and tell him the truth nevertheless'), he complained about the way the Soviet Union was misrepresented by the West. There had been great advances in education and literacy since the Revolution. If the people lacked consumer goods it was because the state had to concentrate on heavy industry. Though Russia was not against arms control, its nuclear strength meant that it feared no one.

> 'We would withstand the onslaught of all the aggressors, however united they were. We are not afraid of the devil himself. And all this has been created by the hands of the people. We do not want to boast of having built an H-Bomb, but had we not done so there might have been a war.'

Stating at great length the Soviet desire for disarmament but doubts about the efficacy of arms control, he blamed the British and the French for not supporting Russia in 1939. Both George Brown and Nye Bevan made clear their unhappiness at this dubious argument, but Khrushchev was in no mood to be interrupted:

> 'See what guests you have. Very soon the policeman will come in again,' he warned them (a reference to the officer giving the traditional cry of 'Who goes home?' earlier in the evening).

When George Brown tried to ask about the pact between Hitler and Stalin, the Russian rebuked him. 'You are still young... I shall reach the question of the other pact. You must not be so impatient.'

He made it clear that he was criticising not the people of Britain and France but the politicians of 1939, like the British Prime Minister Neville Chamberlain:

> 'After all he flew to Munich, not to Moscow, and the alternatives we were faced with were either to fight Hitler on our own or to find some other way out, so we decided to conclude a treaty with Hitler.'

He finished his speech with a warning about the dangers of re-arming Germany:

> 'You might have to pay for that later on. God preserve us from that again.'

The atmosphere was highly charged as Hugh Gaitskell, the Labour Party leader, rose to reply. Choosing his words with care he thanked the two guests for their speeches, but reminded them that the British Labour Party had opposed Neville Chamberlain and helped bring about his downfall. He tried to shift the discussion to the present day, in particular the plight of social democrats being held as political prisoners in Eastern Europe (I had a list in my pocket, ready to produce when the time was right). Gaitskell also expressed concern over the treatment of the Jewish community in Russia.

Unfortunately Khrushchev again lost his temper:

> 'We are not in a position to receive this list. We have been and remain Communists. We shall fight the enemies of the working class and irrespective of whether he is an external or internal enemy he shall be punished if he raises his hand against the working class. And we shall not of course tolerate any interference in the internal affairs of our country.'

> 'We do not seek agreement by going back on our principles. We wish to be loyal Marxists. You have never accepted Marxism and we have never accepted your doctrine. As for the anti-Semitism, that is the reporting of the capitalist press. We must repudiate these charges. That is all.'

> 'What about the social democrats?' asked one of his hearers.

> 'There are no social democrats in the Soviet Union. Some of them have died but the majority have entered the Communist Party. Poland and Czechoslovakia are independent countries and they must not be approached.'

At this point my friend Sam Watson, the miners' leader, intervened:

> 'As one working class member of the British Labour Party to a working class member of the Russian Communist Party – is your party in this era of co-existence prepared to give the same rights to social democrats as it claims for itself?'

'We have one Communist Party,' he responded, 'and we have no intention of setting up a social democratic one.'

After this unsatisfactory answer Nye Bevan tried again:

> 'If we provide Comrade Khrushchev with a list of persons we regard as social democrats, who are in prison in Russia or in countries under the influence of Russia, would we understand that the Comrade would intervene on our behalf?'

'I have already answered that,' he protested.

'You did not reply. We understand that Comrade Khrushchev says these are enemies of the working class but we do not believe they are. Can they leave these countries if they cannot enjoy freedom there?'

Again the Russian resorted to a history lesson, this time speaking about the day in 1918 when members of the Socialist Revolutionary Party killed Moses Uritsky and tried to assassinate Lenin:

'They were enemies and we fought them. There are none of them in our country now.'

Nye persisted, and I pleaded the case for political prisoners in Latvia, Lithuania and Estonia. Khrushchev's fury became menacing:

'You give a very bad impression. We have been following our own path and we can assure you that the time will come when your children will follow in the same path.'

There was a chorus of dissent, to which he retorted, 'It is better to fight for socialism without allies like you.'

George Brown questioned where the socialism was in that argument, but the chairman Edwin Gooch hastily brought the dinner to a close in the mildest possible way.

'We have had a most interesting evening. We hope that the conversation will be continued. Here's to the next meeting.'

'But without me.' Khrushchev had the final word.

Inevitably the press got to hear about the events of the meal, though some of the published accounts were far removed from the truth. At its meeting on the 25th April, Labour's National Executive discussed how to placate the Soviet leaders so that they might be readier to consider the plight of social democrats behind the Iron Curtain. In the end it was decided that Hugh Gaitskell (leader), Jim Griffiths (deputy leader), Edwin Gooch (treasurer) and I should ask for further conversation with the Russians.

Fortunately the Soviets agreed, and a meeting was held at Claridge's Hotel. The atmosphere was calmer but the Soviet leaders were angry that British newspapers had reported in detail the proceedings of a private dinner. They accused the 'Labour press' of suggesting that the two Russians were at odds with each other and that Khrushchev had refused to speak about social democrats in general rather than about political prisoners. Of course we did not escape blame. Khrushchev charged us with 'using the language of Dulles', alluding to the Americans' hard-line Secretary of State. Furthermore he felt that the dinner was a set-up.

'I have not had an audience like that for 37 years, when we had a number of dissidents in the Soviet Union', he exclaimed, 'It was our impression that the dinner was planned in advance and specific roles allocated. No one tried to stop Mr George Brown, who was insolent. Our impression was that he was instructed, and no-one told him to quieten down.'

He expressed regret that it was easier to deal with the Conservatives than with Labour:

'We want more solidarity. We do not complain about our treatment. That is transient and we are prepared to seek contacts with you. In the first place it will be on questions of peace. We would like it to be widened later.'

Hugh Gaitskell, whilst rejecting his wilder assertions, welcomed the idea of further discussions. Again he tried to raise the issue of social democrats who were political prisoners. Khrushchev, as before, changed the subject and spoke about Neville Chamberlain. Jim Griffiths, a senior figure in our Party, issued a dignified reminder that Labour had opposed Chamberlain and had been active in his removal from office.

At this point Hugh Gaitskell felt that both sides had expressed their views fully and there was no point in continuing. He thanked the Russians for agreeing to meet us. But Khrushchev had not finished:

'If you become the next government, your policies may not be helpful to the Soviet Union.'

'You must remove that impression from your mind', I told him, 'The British Labour Movement is unanimous in its desire for better relations with the Soviet Union, and a Labour government would act on that basis. I hope the Soviet Union would reciprocate in a like spirit.'

Surprisingly, the meeting ended in quite a cordial atmosphere, and Khrushchev invited me to discuss with Mr Malik the possibility of a Labour delegation visiting the Soviet Union.

There was a bizarre incident a fortnight later. A Romanian called Traian Cercega told the press that he was 'well and enjoying full liberty' and not in a Russian gaol. This was an obvious attempt to discredit the list of imprisoned social democrats that Hugh Gaitskell tried to give Khruschev. Since the Soviets had refused to take the list, how did they know that Cercega was included? The list was still in my safe. Only Gaitskell and I knew the names and we had not given the information to anyone else.

The only good thing about the whole affair was that it revealed to the British public and to socialist parties in other countries the vast gulf between Communism and democratic socialism. As Khrushchev had put it:

'I'm not inviting you to take up Marxism because you would be very poor Marxists – and we would be awful Labour Party members.'

* * *

Anna Kéthly speaks

The most moving session of the Socialist International that I ever attended took place in Vienna from the 2nd-6th July 1957. Anna Kéthly had left Hungary the previous year during its brief period of freedom in order to speak on behalf of the Nagy Government. Forbidden to return, she addressed the International and gave a detailed indictment of the application of Soviet Communism and a warning for those who believed that the end justifies the means:

'They think that dictatorship is an inevitable, necessary evil without which transition from an inhumane to a humane and classless society, free from exploitation and worthy of human dignity, is not possible... All that it achieved in Hungary was to obscure the difference between capitalist and totalitarian exploitation.'

Later she revealed what it was like for a socialist under a communist dictatorship:

'We spent many years in prison. Even when we were released later on we were still behind the Iron Curtain. For us it was one of the most depressing experiences that in the free world, on the other side of the Iron Curtain, the achievements of the Labour movement were frequently taken for granted. What was a most pleasant surprise for us, coming from a country behind the Iron Curtain, is regarded by those who live beyond it as a matter of course, and in consequence is not sufficiently valued. We know better. Freedom, as Matteotti said, is like air; we can only appreciate its full worth when we are deprived of it.'

She concluded by begging us not to forget Hungary:

'If the free world sinks into apathy and indifference over the sufferings of a small satellite state, then it is also forgetting that the Hungarian Revolution in its struggle against dictatorship gave the free world the highest example, and rendered it an invaluable service.'

This was the last conference of the Socialist International under my Chairmanship. After six years in office it would have been unfair for me

Anna Kéthly   *Dedication on reverse of picture*

to continue. Not only were there able socialists from other countries who would be extremely useful to the Executive, but the British Labour Movement contained men and women whose contributions to the International were, of necessity, limited while I held the highest office. Alsing Anderson of Denmark succeeded me as Chairman, and the British leader Hugh Gaitskell became the third Vice-Chairman.

✳ ✳ ✳

Israel

Israel's geographical position allows its Labour Movement to participate in the European scene and to contribute to the new and vigorous socialism of Asia.

I met many remarkable people there, like Reuven Barkatt, the General Secretary of Mapai (the Labour Party). He previously headed the political department of Histadrut, the General Federation of Jewish Labour, which plays an important role in social services, in the ownership of industry and in government affairs.

I first visited Israel in the summer of 1953 as the guest of Mapai and Histadrut. Invited to speak at a public meeting in Jerusalem, I told my hosts how impressed I had been by the Israeli delegate at the Asian Socialist Conference in India, and I urged them to play a significant part in bridging the gap between the socialism of Europe and that of Asia, so that one day there could be fusion of the Socialist International and the

Asian organisation. The Jerusalem branch of Mapai held a reception for me, where I had the pleasure of meeting Golda Myerson, the Minister of Labour. Later I dined with the Acting Premier Moshe Sharett, and was received by President Ben-Zvi.

On my second visit I was accompanied by my wife Norah, and we made many more contacts.

My special memory is of Prime Minister David Ben-Gurion. He was in hospital recovering from a bombing incident in the Knesset (Parliament), and we found his bed in the corner of a public ward. Dressed in hospital pyjamas, he was receiving the same treatment as any other patient. David was very cheerful despite his nerve-shattering experience, and his eyes twinkled when he greeted us:

Morgan, his wife, Reuven Barkatt

'I'm glad the British Labour Party are on such good terms with us. I only hope they feel the same way when they are in government.'

Our meeting brought home to us the wit, the wisdom and the humility of this great socialist.

* * *

Latin America

Although no longer Chairman of the Socialist International, I remained a member of the Bureau, the main administrative committee, and I kept in touch with all my old friends. In February 1960, on behalf of the

International, I undertook an extensive tour of Latin America to consider the nature of left wing parties there. I knew that they were few in number and relatively weak. Only Argentina and Uruguay had affiliated to the International, and Uruguay had just resigned in protest at the French socialist policy on Algeria.

A Latin American Secretariat set up by the International had established contacts with a wide variety of democratic parties but had not persuaded any to affiliate to the parent body. Many of these were anti-dictatorship, anti-imperialist, democratic and nationalist, and determined to protect the development of their own natural resources. For them, imperialism was not the last stage of capitalism but the beginning of their struggle for liberation.

Mexico had no socialist party at national level. The Partido Revolucionario Institucional, a coalition of conservative and radical democrats, was far and away the most influential group in the country. In the 1930s under President Lazaro Cardenas the party had instituted its own New Deal, and in the most recent Presidential Election (1958) their candidate had polled 6,769,754 votes out of 7,485,000. I saw welcome signs that the party's left wing (in which Lazaro Cardenas was still active) was playing a greater role in policy and organisation. Significantly, I was asked many questions about the British Labour Party's theories and methods.

There were two small socialist groups in Mexico; one Spanish, the other German. The Spanish had a thousand members, the majority in Mexico City. The veteran Indalecio Prieto was the group's leader.

From Mexico I moved on to Cuba. At the time of his triumph in January 1959, Castro had been committed to a far reaching revolutionary programme: land distribution, reform of national and local government, the freeing of Cuba from US tutelage and effective planning to end the colonial one crop economy. The land reform had brought the regime into conflict not only with the big Cuban landowners but also with various North American companies who worked the sugar estates.

Castro's revolution had been widely acclaimed by Latin American radicals like Rómulo Betancourt, the Prime Minister of Venezuela. José Figueres Ferrer, the former President of Costa Rica, gave his approval to the new regime in Cuba but publicly criticised Castro for his ferociously anti-American stance. The new Cuban government was planning to create a Latin American trades union congress rather than join the International Congress of Free Trades Union, or its Communist counterpart, the WFTU. However, several leaders of Castro's 26th July Movement told me they wanted close contact with the Socialist

International and with the British Labour Party, and students from the Havana University hoped to exchange ideas with the International Union of Socialist Youth.

My next stop was Venezuela, a country producing nearly three times as much oil as Kuwait. Following the free elections of 1958, Rómulo Betancourt of Acción Democrática had formed a coalition government that was pursuing a policy not far removed from democratic socialism. There was widespread hostility towards the USA, as dramatically illustrated by the treatment of Vice President Richard Nixon when he visited the country. There was a ubiquitous fear that the former dictator Jiménez, now resident in Miami, would force his way back to power. I attended an anniversary demonstration and learnt subsequently that a number of people there had been arrested and found to be in possession of hand grenades.

In Panama I found a small but enthusiastic Socialist Party led by Dr Demetrio Porras. I also had the exhilarating experience of addressing an audience of peasants outside Panama City. The meeting was keen and enthusiastic, but the party's influence was clearly limited.

Arriving in Costa Rica I was met by 'Don Pepe' Figueres, the leading figure in the National Liberation Movement. Unlike many popular leaders in South America, he firmly believed in the need for economic, political and cultural exchange with the United States, provided that it was on a basis of equality. He was also actively establishing and maintaining contact with like-minded parties in other parts of Latin America. His vigorous opposition to all dictatorships caused him to clash with the conservative President Mario Echandi Jiménez, who was eager for better relations with Luis Somoza, the dictator of Nicaragua.

After Costa Rica I hoped to visit Ecuador, until I heard that the left-wing party there had just split between those who wished to work with the Communists and those who did not. As it would have been wrong to get involved in a local dispute, I changed my plans and visited Peru, only to find controversy there too. The Alianza Popular Revolucionaria Americana had previously been regarded as the true radical party, but was now accused of fascism by the Peruvian Socialist Party and by many in Latin America.

My next call was La Paz, Bolivia, where I attended the Conference of the Latin American Secretariat. The host party, the Movimento Nacionalista Revolucionario, had been in power since the revolution of 1952. It received most of its support from the highland Indians, many of them tin-miners. As the price of tin had halved in five years the nationalisation of the mines had not brought all the expected benefits, but it was still a notable achievement.

There was an interesting situation in Chile. The Communist Party had been prohibited from taking part in elections since 1947, but had kept its organisation intact, so that it was in a strong position to bargain with other parties. Both the Socialists and the middle-class Radicals had flirted with the banned party. The Chilean Government, which represented various sections of the Spanish aristocracy, was seeking to make such pacts illegal in order to reduce the chances of a left-wing victory.

The Argentine Socialist Party was as old as the British Labour Party but had lost a lot of its working-class supporters during the Peron regime. After Peron's fall in 1955, the Socialists had to win back the workers. Inevitably, there was a split between those who favoured co-operation with the Peronists and those strongly opposed to the idea.

The government was in the hands of the right-wing President Arturo Frondizi, who was subject to constant pressure from the army. When I was there, a government spokesman admitted that its economic policy was unpopular, and that the Peronists had the best propaganda. This was brought home to me when I saw the local election results, in which Peron's supporters left their cards blank:

Blank votes	2,086,103
Opposition	2,060014
Government	1,782,912

In Uruguay, the Blanco Party, mainly composed of descendents of the Spanish aristocracy, had just wrested power from the Colorado Party, which had been in government for no less than 93 years. The main factor contributing to the Colorados' defeat was the economic crisis due to the falling price of exports, especially wool. The same situation had also created a wave of anti-American feeling, which manifested itself in a student demonstration during a visit by President Eisenhower.

The Uruguayan Socialist Party was very small, with barely a thousand members and only three deputies in a Chamber of 99, but I was grateful for the chance to urge a return to membership of the Socialist International. From the reactions to my speech to the party's executive, I gleaned that the younger members believed in a Yugoslav brand of socialism.

Brazil was the final country on my tour and by far the largest in South America, with a population of nearly 60 million. Politically it was democratic, though a few restrictions remained; the Communist Party had been banned since 1947. Of the four main groups, the Labour Party and the Social Democrats had a Peron-style policy of state intervention in industry, the National Democratic Union drew its support from the middle-class voters with financial interests, and the Socialist Party led by Vellasco was a young organisation with little influence so far. I gathered that older members of the Labour Party and the Socialists were keen to work together, but that the younger colleagues were vigorously opposed to any moves in that direction.

Morgan in Brazil

There seemed to be no racial conflict, but the apparent inability of all the parties to solve the country's serious economic problems resulted in widespread dissatisfaction. In the Sao Paulo state elections a female rhino named Cacareco topped the poll in several districts, because so few voters felt able to support the official candidates.

Many countries in Latin America were keen to work with British businessmen, but too many opportunities were wasted. In Panama, efforts to persuade British firms to work in the canal area had failed completely. Brazil already had French, German and American car factories, and imported vehicles could not compete. British car companies were looking for local agents but not for service stations, whereas their North American counterparts established service depots first, knowing that the cars would then sell themselves. United Kingdom textile manufacturers in Peru had to import Swiss equipment. Our private enterprise, supposedly so efficient, chose to neglect this emerging sub-continent.

Appendix

Marxism and the British Labour Party

My speech in June 1950 to the International Socialist Conference in Copenhagen caused so much controversy back home that the left-wing magazine *Tribune* (9th June 1950) published the entire text 'so that readers can make their own judgment on what Morgan Phillips actually said.'

I reproduce the speech below:

> Though the British Labour Party is widely known and much discussed, the main source of its inspiration and its ethical appeal is not understood by many of our comrades in other countries.
>
> British socialism owes little to Karl Marx either in theory or practice, or in its methods of organising the working class. Trotsky was not far wrong when he said that the English Revolution brought about by the Puritans was nourished on Biblical texts, the French Revolution on the abstractions of democracy, and the Russian Revolution on Marxism.
>
> 'The Russian revolutionary party', wrote Trotsky, 'which was to place its stamp upon a whole epoch, sought an expression for the tasks of the revolution neither in the Bible nor in the secularised Christianity called pure democracy, but in the material relations of the social classes.'
>
> Marx, as we know (and not merely because Lenin told us), was profoundly influenced in the development of his teaching by German philosophy, English political economy and the social implications of the French Revolution. Marx's economics, as well as his politics, were challenged and finally renounced by the founders and teachers of the British Labour Party.
>
> Fabian socialism parted company with Marxism at the point where the controversy arose as to what constituted 'value'. Instead of the labour theory of value, the Fabians built upon the marginal theory of value formulated by the English economist Jevons. Value of a thing, according to this theory, is measured not by the socially necessary labour it contains, but by the utility of the thing at the margin of supply where the law of indifference comes in to determine its exchange value. It is the final utility of the thing, not the identical quantity of socially necessary labour embodied in it, which determines its exchange against another thing, with money as the medium.
>
> All this of course is elementary. But rejection by the British socialists of the Marxist theory of value had important practical consequences in the development of the politically organised labour movement, because of the interaction between Marx's economic thinking and his theory of politics, based upon his historical materialism and his doctrine of the class struggle.

Marx's conception of the political organisation required for the waging of the class war was not adopted by the British labour movement.

British socialism has pointed the way to the achievement of that rarest phenomenon in history – a revolutionary change in political control without physical conflict. It promises, moreover, the attainment of a planned economy in which proletarian exploitation is not tolerated, and where the fundamental freedoms of the individual citizen, worker and wage earner are safeguarded.

The Marxist theory of proletarian dictatorship as the prelude to Communism leads to what Trotsky calls the militarisation of labour and state compulsion.

Socialism, he said, will remain an empty sound without militarisation and state compulsion of labour. 'There is no way to socialise except by the authoritative regulation of economic forces and resources … and the centralised distribution of labour in harmony with the general state plan.'

This is the essential point of divergence between Marxian socialism and British socialism. It would be true to say that British socialism has never lost its ethical inspiration. This goes back of course far beyond Marx. Marxian socialism disdains any ethical or utopian interpretation. There is barely a trace of any human emotion in Marx's writings. But the writings from which British socialists drew their inspiration, even to the present generation, are filled with such sentiments as are contained in this quotation from the *Utopia* of Sir Thomas More:

'To speak plainly my free sentiments I must freely own that as long as there is any property, and while money is the standard of all other things, I cannot think that any nation can be governed either justly or happily; not justly, because the best things will fall to the share of the worst men; nor happily, because all things will be divided among a few (and even those are not in all respects happy), the rest being left to be absolutely miserable … From whence I am persuaded, that till property is taken away there can be no equitable or just distribution of things, nor can the world be happily governed: for as long as that is maintained, the greatest and the far best part of mankind will be still oppressed with a load of cares and anxieties.'

Such is the note that rings persistently and clearly in the writings of the pre-Marxian socialists. And nowhere more than in these writings are the evils arising out of the institution of private property, the existence of an unproductive class, the misdistribution and misuse of wealth, the domination of money, the exploitation of the poor by the rich and even the indictment of the state as the managing committee of the rich more emphatically exposed and condemned.

British socialists do not consider it at all a reproach or a source of weakness in their intellectual and political position that their movement has been profoundly influenced by religious thought. The very organisation of our British working class movement embodies methods we have taken over from religious institutions. It is not only the Christian Socialists of an earlier day who have left their impress upon the thought and the teaching of British socialists. Methods of religious organisation arising out of the evangelical revival of the 18th Century were incorporated in the organisation of the radical societies, the political associations, the trade unions and the friendly societies which throve apace in the 19ᵗʰ Century. When Chartism revived after its defeat in 1839, its reorganisation as a national movement owed a great deal to radicals and democrats who belonged to the Methodist Church.

The National Charter Association formed at that time was in fact founded upon a system of 'classes' borrowed from the Methodist form of organisation. In the later Chartist Movement, under the direction of a general council and a central executive, committee adherents and supporters of the movement were formed into 'classes'. Each class was composed of ten members under the supervision of a leader appointed by the executive committee. But there is a world of difference in the spirit and the purpose of this kind of class organisation and leadership and that of the Communist cell.

It is a fact too that the British labour movement, both on its trade union and on its political side, drew heavily upon the religious communities. The Methodist and other churches carried on their work not so much by a paid ministry but by the service of volunteer laymen, who occupied the pulpits as lay preachers (local preachers as they were called), served as officers in the church and teachers in their Sunday schools. The doctrinal basis of Methodism and the English Free Churches generally encouraged democratic ideas and sympathies, and it was a natural evolution of the laymen in these churches to assume responsibilities of leadership in the friendly societies, the trade unions and the political associations that were the early 'carriers' of the ethical ideals of socialism before the British Socialist Societies, as such were founded in the last two decades of the 19ᵗʰ Century.

Without overemphasising the significance of these religious influences in the making of the British labour movement, one can recall the ethical movement out of which the Fabian Society emerged, along with the Labour Church movement and the Independent Labour Party.

The essential point is that Marxism as a philosophy of materialism, as an economic theory and as a form of political organisation with revolutionary intention and aim is historically an aberrant tendency in the development of British socialism.

Trotsky called reformist socialism – an opprobrious phrase on his lips – as the leftward shadow of professorial liberalism. If, by 'reformist socialism' the reference is to British socialism, it is much more than a shadow; it is the living embodiment of an ethical inspiration, and of ideas about democratic organisation and methods which contradict Marxism at almost every living point.

Welcome to the Socialist International

by Julius Braunthal

This article by the Secretary of Comisco was published in the April 1951 edition of *Fact*, and is reprinted by kind permission of the Labour Party.

A Historic Act

The day was cold, bitter. Smith Square was deserted. For once the bombed church in the centre seemed to dominate the surrounding office blocks; they too had become shells. Two or three hours before, their workers had drained into the residential parts of the city, where by now they were packed into football stadiums or jostling in the city centres. The spate of traffic over Lambeth Bridge had dwindled to an occasional bus that could be heard far away, unexpectedly noisy as it carried two or three late workers home. But one room in all this wilderness of offices was busy with voices, though even there a Saturday afternoon airiness could be felt.

A Belgian MP was making a speech in a gathering of some forty persons from Austria, Belgium, Britain, Canada, Chile, Denmark, Finland, France, Germany, Greece, Holland, Italy, Japan, Luxemburg, Norway, Poland, Spain, Sweden, Switzerland, Trieste and Yugoslavia. Those who could understand French listened appreciatively but not intently for they knew everything that the Belgian was going to say. The others waited, bored, for the translations and when, in huddles at opposite ends of the conference table, the interpreters began urgently murmuring their paraphrases, those who had understood sank in their turn listlessly into their chairs. At length one of the interpreters finished and sat back. His class quietly broke up, joining the unoccupied majority, who doodled or yawned or stared vacantly at the window, through which only brick walls were to be seen. For a little time the second interpreter hurried sibilantly over his concluding sentences like a man who had lost a race, then he too leaned back.

After a moment to make sure that the interpreters had finally stopped speaking, an Englishman rose. For a few minutes he spoke clearly, strongly; then the furtive whisperings of the interpreters set in again. After the Englishman, a Dutchman; then an Italian; then a Norwegian; then a Frenchman; then others, others; each followed by the subdued, hasty confidences of the interpreters. At last the chairman perfunctorily put the resolution to the meeting, glancing from face to face with lacklustre eye. None of the delegates appeared to vote; they allowed their support to be taken for granted. Here an Austrian stubbed out a cigarette, the ashtray nagging the table like a cat scraping at a window pane; then the Frenchman closed his notebook with a decisive snap, and shot it into his pocket. But just for a moment, all eyes rested on the chairman. He was a distinguished French journalist, short, plump, bald, with a fringe of dark hair. With a smile and a gesture which seemed to mean, 'Ah well, we've done it', he cleared his throat as if he felt that something ought to be said, but said nothing. Then with a swift action he reached over for his agenda. There was a rustle of papers all round the table as the conference turned to the next business. The Socialist International had been reborn.

* * *

A change of name

It might be truer to describe the decision taken at Transport House (Westminster, London, England) on the 3rd March as a change of name rather than a rebirth. What had happened was that the curiously named Comisco had resolved that its parent conference should assume the historic dignity of the International.

In May 1946 the Labour Party organised an International Socialist Conference at Clacton, which was followed at half-yearly intervals by conferences at Bournemouth, Zurich, Antwerp, Vienna, Berne and Copenhagen (June 1950). At Antwerp in December 1947 the Conference decided to appoint an executive committee to meet more frequently and to deal in detail with current problems. This is the Committee of the International Conference, Comisco for short. Comisco's decision on the 3rd March to revive the title of The International is subject to confirmation by the full Conference at Frankfurt in July. It is proposed that Comisco itself will then be renamed the Council of the Socialist International.

* * *

Strength

How strong is the new International? At the beginning of this year some 33 parties were affiliated, representing 10 million fee-paying members and 44 million votes received at the most recent elections. This is a much greater strength than that of the famous Second International, which in its last report, published in 1931, claimed 6.25 million members and 26.5 million votes.

These totals underestimate the real strength of the new International, as several of the affiliated parties are not in a position to reveal membership figures. These include the Socialist Parties of Argentina, Bulgaria, Czechoslovakia, Greece, Hungary, Poland and Spain, among others, all of which are represented. By far the biggest adherent is the British Labour Party, with over 5 million members and over 13 million votes. The twelve most successful parties electorally are:

Country	Members (000)	Votes (000)	Per cent total vote
Sweden	700	1817	49.1
Britain	5422	13296	46.4
Norway	203	801	46
Denmark	295	813	39.6
Austria	616	1624	38.8
Israel	–	155	35
Belgium	132	1705	34.5
West Germany	736	6934	29.2
Finland	100	495	26.3
Switzerland	53	258	26.3
Holland	110	1244	25.7
Japan	100	7316	25.5

In addition to these, the Party in the Western Zone of Berlin polled 44.7% of the votes, and in the Saar 32.8%. A disappointing figure is that for the United States, where the Socialist Party claims only 30,000 members and 140,000 votes, or one vote in 300. In Canada, the Cooperative Commonwealth Federation polled 13.4% of the total.

Three of the parties in the International form the governments of their countries, namely Britain, Norway and Sweden. Six participate in coalitions: Austria, Denmark, France, Italy, Israel and Switzerland. In addition, the German Socialists control several provincial governments and the Canadian CCF controls the Province of Saskatchewan.

* * *

How it works

Comisco meets three times a year to receive reports and to make broad decisions of policy. At the March Conference, for example, reports were presented by Van der Goes (Holland) on European Unity, by Denis Healey (Britain) on European Defence and by Mme Kisnel-Brutochy on a recent Women's Conference; a statement was made by Ryoichi Oka on the position of the Japanese party, and resolutions were cast denouncing oppression in Argentina and in Greece, deploring the reprieve of Nazi war criminals and demanding the continued exclusion of Spain from the Atlantic Pact.

Detailed work is done by Experts Conferences, of which six have been held in little over two years, by Special Commissions and Study Groups. The Economic Experts have held five Conferences: on techniques for administering nationalised industries, on problems of European economic co-operation, on workers' participation in industrial management, on international control of basic industries and on the liberalisation of trade. The sixth Experts Conference was on propaganda and organisation. One of the Special Commissions is drafting a statement of the Principles of Democratic Socialism under the Chairmanship of Guy Mollet, Secretary of the French Party.

Comisco is also beginning to assist the activities of the Socialist Delegates to the Council of Europe.

Decisions of the International are not binding on its members. The resolution passed on the 3rd March said:

> 'Socialist co-operation must be based on consent. The resolutions passed by an international socialist body must reflect common agreement freely reached. They cannot constitute a binding command on parties which are individually responsible to their own members and to a national electorate. In this it has learnt the lessons of the past.'

A double loyalty

The fact is that so long as national states exist and the citizen's prosperity is bound up with that of his country, especially if he enjoys voting rights, progressive persons will always feel a divided or rather a double loyalty: to their countries and to international ideals such as socialism. It is particularly important that the Socialist International should not have binding authority over its members when several of its members are governments of their countries. So long as the world itself is not federated there can be no federation of national parties, unless their object is to overthrow their respective states in the interests of a national system, as is the case with Cominform. Even the Communist International could not function as an authoritarian body if it was not dominated by the Russian Communist Party at the same time as the nations with Communist governments are dominated by the Soviet Government. Thus the relationship of parties in the International conforms to the relationship of their governments outside it. If the one is dependent, the other can be dependent; but if the one is independent the other must be likewise. The strength of the 1951 Socialist International is that it recognises this elementary truth

Julius Braunthal

* * *

The Socialist International Declaration

Socialists work for a world of peace and freedom, for a world in which the exploitation and enslavement of men by men and peoples by peoples is unknown.

For a world in which the development of the individual personality is the basis for the fruitful development of mankind.

They appeal to the solidarity of all working men in the struggle for this great aim.

Declaration of the First Congress of the Socialist International, Frankfurt-am-Main, 30ᵗʰ June-3ʳᵈ July 1951

* * *

Socialist International's 2ⁿᵈ Congress
at the Palazzo Reale, Milan 17ᵗʰ-21ˢᵗ October 1951
Extract from the opening address by Morgan Phillips:

It is fitting that we should be holding our Congress in this city of Milan, which has been the birthplace and the centre of Italian socialism ever since the great Italian socialist leader Filippo Turati formed the Lega Socialista Milanese more than 69 years ago.

It was here that the forces of reaction launched their attack in the notorious four days of Milan ... Throughout the long years of fascist oppression by Mussolini's Blackshirts, we knew that our Italian comrades would fight on. Our belief was vindicated when Mussolini was overthrown and a strong Italian Socialist Party emerged once more to take the lead in resistance to Nazi occupation, and to inspire a new Risorgimento. We rejoice to see the Italian Democratic Socialist Party united once more and freed from the deadly embrace of the Communists and their fellow travellers, leading the Italian workers in our common struggle for the victory of International Socialism. For Filippo Turati

167

there were two cardinal points: that socialism must be democratic, and that democratic socialism must be united. They are still the basis of socialism in Italy. They are the basis of socialism in all our countries. They are the basis of the Socialist International. Long live the PSDI. Long live the Socialist International.

* * *

The Socialist International's 3rd Congress
Stockholm 15th – 18th July 1953

Part of the Chairman's address by Morgan Phillips:

Our meeting here in the home of Sweden's Parliament is not only an example of the well-known generosity of Swedish hospitality, but it is also symbolic. It symbolises our conviction that socialism and democracy are indivisible.

Without socialism there cannot be true democracy; without democracy there cannot be socialism. The truth of this is nowhere more clearly demonstrated than in Sweden. In the British Labour Party we have a system of what we call refresher courses, which are schools to which our experienced party organisers go from time to time in order to get back to first principles. For many of us from other countries, this visit to Sweden is something like a refresher course. Here we feel we are getting back to the basic principles of democratic socialism …

The unity and strength which has been built up in the non-Communist world over the past few years is no mean achievement. Co-operation is paying dividends and will continue to do so. Our common objective has been to secure independence and liberty, and the USA has made a great contribution towards that objective. It is upon these twin principles of independence and liberty that our co-operation has been based. Let me say frankly that the whole structure is in danger of being undermined by the growth of witch-hunting in the USA, with Senator McCarthy as the Grand Inquisitor. The free world has come to mean those countries that cherish liberty and practise democracy. If in the United States McCarthyism were to succeed in making it a mockery, one of its pillars would be uprooted and the whole edifice would be shaken to its foundations.

The Socialist International's 4th Congress
In London 12th-16th July 1955

Extract from the opening address by Morgan Phillips:

Already the influence we can exercise on international affairs – directly as parties and collectively as the International – is considerable. As an indication of this, and of the close attention we accord to international developments, I would point to the five conferences on international affairs that have been held, notably those in Brussels immediately after the end of the Berlin Conference, and in Vienna during the Geneva Conference.

These conferences went a long way to clarify and crystallise the attitude of the International Socialist movement to the current problems. Here in London we are again to formulate the policy of the social democratic movement at a point in history which might well mark the end of one phase and the beginning of a new one in international relations.

His closing statement at the end of the Congress:

In my opinion it has been a helpful Congress. For the first time all sessions have been held in public – which explains perhaps the lack of interest shown by the press, who are usually very keen to report on sessions held in private. Important declarations have been adopted and greater unity and greater understanding have been reached. The International can now go forward to new conquests in other parts of the world, adding to its strength and vigour as a movement.

I thank you all for your co-operation. In particular I thank our Asian comrades for coming such a long way to attend the Congress. In the very near future at least a Council conference should be held outside Europe, to demonstrate the desire for closer unity with comrades in other countries and the determination to weld one single worldwide socialist organisation, which will carry forward the banner of democratic socialism.

The Socialist International's 5ᵗʰ Congress
In Vienna 2ⁿᵈ-5ᵗʰ July 1957

Extract from the address of Alsing Andersen (Chairman Elect):

In taking over the Chairmanship from our good friend Morgan Phillips I would first like to say a few hearty words of thanks to him for the many years he has served as Chairman of the International.

Even before the end of the Second World War the British Labour Party was the natural centre for the democratic socialist parties who wanted to rebuild the Socialist International. We who remember the years immediately after the war know how indebted our parties are to the British Labour Party – and to Morgan Phillips.

As Chairman during those years, Morgan Phillips has been a central figure in the reconstruction of the Socialist International, and I feel I am in complete agreement with Congress in extending to you our most sincere thanks. We value not only your work but also your personal friendship.

As you come from Wales I shall not venture to call you English. But at least you are British, and for us foreigners – or perhaps I should say aliens – you are an Englishman with English common sense and English honour, and I am sure that we are all looking forward to meeting you again in our common work.

Extract from the concluding speech by Morgan Phillips:

One cannot help feeling with regret the loss of many good comrades who joined us in our work: Hans Hedtoft, Louis Levy, Salomon Grumbach, Louis de Brouckère and many others who helped to mould the character, ideology and structure of the movement.

In 1951 we were able to agree on a declaration of aims and tasks. Since then we have had six years' experience. We have welcomed many new parties. We have seen the growth of the Asian Socialist Conference. We have seen the establishment of the Latin American Secretariat. I believe we have very great opportunities for expansion in the future.

We in Britain are seeking to build the same kind of contacts within the Commonwealth, to stimulate and develop parties which accept the democratic socialist faith and join with us in the great socialist family. These things are important especially when sometimes we feel exhausted by the strain of day-to-day work in our own countries.

It is good to sit back and reflect on the progress that has been made in the development of this organisation. Now you have a new Secretary and a new Chairman. I think it is a good thing to have changes. I myself look forward to the time when I shall be sitting among the delegates, seeking to catch the eye of the Chairman, and then proceeding to speak not in the undertones of impartiality imposed by chairmanship, but in the overtones of a party that has been triumphant in its own country.

We have for half a century been urging the establishment of a welfare state, public ownership of industry, full employment and social security. In spite of the progress we have made in Britain, as in many other countries, hundreds of millions of people are today deprived of liberty. We must give leadership on a worldwide scale, and if we join hands and work together with an ever-greater effort, we shall be able to play our part in shaping the world according to our ideas.

ARCHITECT or BEE?

The Human Price of Technology

Mike Cooley

Introduction by

Frances O'Grady

www.spokesmanbooks.com